INTRODUCTION TO LOCAL AREA NETWORKS

INTRODUCTION TO LOCAL AREA NETWORKS

JUDSON MIERS

THOMSON
™
DELMAR LEARNING   Australia · Canada · Mexico · Singapore · Spain · United Kingdom · United States

Introduction to Local Area Networks
Judson Miers

Vice President, Technology and Trades ABU:
David Garza

Director of Learning Solutions:
Sandy Clark

Senior Acquisitions Editor:
Stephen Helba

Development:
Dawn Daugherty

Marketing Director:
Deborah S. Yarnell

Channel Manager:
Dennis Williams

Marketing Coordinator:
Stacey Wiktorek

Production Director:
Patty Stephan

Senior Production Manager:
Larry Main

Production Editor:
Benj Gleeksman

Library of Congress Cataloging-in-Publication Data:

Miers, Judson.
   Introduction to local area networks / Judson Miers.
      p. cm.
   Includes index.
   ISBN-13: 978-1-4180-0058-5
   ISBN-10: 1-4180-0058-2
   1. Local area networks (Computer networks)   I. Title.
   TK5105.7.M534 2007
   004.6'8--dc22

                        2006009352

NOTICE TO THE READER

Contents

Preface

When I began the transition from biologist/chemist to network technician, I was extremely intimidated. It seemed that everything I knew about was in complete opposition to the world of computers and networks. A friend and mentor directed me to Peter Norton's book *Inside the PC*. I found that I could absorb only about 10 pages at a time before my mind was spinning. After several months I had read the entire text. I realized only later that the concepts behind what I knew about biology, chemistry, and mathematics were actually the same concepts but expressed differently. This intimidating new subject was much more approachable once I began to liken it to something I already knew.

Although there are many technically correct and highly acclaimed resources for learning about computer networks, I wanted to write a textbook for those of us who were not originally computer programmers or electrical engineers; a book that actually explains in a real-world setting *how* networks really work. My great-grandfather once told me that if a person "can't tell you so you understand, they're either lying or they don't know either." I have tried to write this text to be approachable—not just for techies but for anyone who needs an overall understanding of networking.

Intended Audience

This text was written as an introduction to local area networks and their design. It is intended to be not a technical reference but rather an introductory text that can be bundled with other texts for their more in-depth and specific technical explanations.

Writing Philosophy

I have always learned better if I have an endpoint in mind before I start. I can appreciate learning in the abstract, but I am more enthusiastic if I know there is a "real" benefit to the lesson. Case studies are more likely to get my attention than esoteric theories. During my time with SkillPath/CompuMaster Seminars, I began to project my way of learning on my students. In fact, my first couple of months presenting computer seminars were horrible because I tried to cover the material in the most effective and academic ways possible. Of course, student boredom quickly overshadowed my good intentions. In a moment of enlightenment, I decided to sprinkle personal anecdotes and case studies into the overall course material. Much to my surprise, my students' satisfaction with my teaching soared!

I took this concept to DeVRY University (formerly DeVRY Institute of Technology) and the University of Kansas Medical Center. I started my network and data communications classes by having the students make up a fictitious company that would be our model organization throughout the term. We would then flesh out the organization and begin to design its network infrastructure. Along the way, we always came to numerous places that took us back to some purely technical discussion about the merits of a specific technology; but the overall meandering course of the term was to design, specify, and build the network that was best suited to the organization, its business needs, and its available budget. From this environment I formed the idea to write this approach in a textbook. The case studies in this text come directly from sample organizations for which my students have performed BTA reports for the past several years. In fact, students often ask me what a "good BTA" looks like or how I would design the network. That's exactly what this textbook discusses. For my past students, here's your chance to critique my work and put it to the test. I hope you enjoy this text as much as I enjoyed teaching and writing it!

The tone of this text is informal. I wrote this text as if I were actually lecturing in a classroom or sitting down with students in a small group. I had my chapters looked over not by colleagues who are my peers but by people who did not have that level of expertise. I wanted this text to be approachable by just about anyone, regardless of experience or training.

Organization of This Book

Part 1—Getting Started lays the foundation and some of the basic technical concepts that comprise local area networking.

Chapter 1—Laying the Foundation: This chapter is a general overview of the rest of the text and the industry overall.

Chapter 2—A Review of the OSI Model: The OSI model was originally designed to help introduce a common language for all networking manufacturers, engineers, technicians, and the like. Because of the artificial nature of this language, it is often difficult to grasp it. This chapter explains the OSI model.

Chapter 3—Network Basics: The chapter begins with a condensed overview of the OSI model before introducing the basic components that make up the network.

Chapter 4—Asset Management: How can you begin to design a network if you don't know what you've already purchased and installed?

Chapter 5—Business and Technology Analysis: Developed by Goldman and Rawlings, the BTA has become a standard for understanding a business or organization's financial goals and how the network can help achieve those goals.

Chapter 6—Computer Professionals Unlimited, Inc.: The business processes of CPU, our fictitious organization, are outlined in this chapter. CPU was begun by a few college friends who decided they wanted to start a different kind of network consulting company to build long-term relationships with their customers.

Part 2—Target Organizations is devoted to the target organizations that will be explored and the networks that will be designed for their business needs. These are the same organizations my students and I developed for use in the local area network classes at DeVRY University.

Chapter 7—Cross Creek Construction: CCC is a small construction company that has been doing all its work on paper. The owner has decided that the company cannot continue to do business as it has in the past if it wants to grow.

Chapter 8—Red Bridge School District: RBSD has just received a sizable grant and has decided to upgrade its existing computers and network to have a state-of-the-art computing facility for its students and faculty.

Chapter 9—CPU's Network: We've seen what types of networks CPU has designed for others; now it's time to see what CPU's network and facilities look like.

Part 3—What Happens Next? is an exploration of maintaining the network, monitoring network traffic, and planning the next upgrade.

Chapter 10—Performing the Installation: This chapter is the culmination of many years of trial -and error, gashed hands, miserable attic climbs, and the like. There are tips and tricks gleaned from both mentors and hard work.

Chapter 11—Checking Network Health: Our new network is installed, but how well is it performing? Without some sort of a baseline, do you know if it's acting normally?

Chapter 12—Planning the Next Upgrade: It's satisfying when you have your new network up and running, but it won't meet the needs of the business forever. How do you plan for the next upgrade?

Chapter 13—Evaluating and Choosing IT Employees, Consultants, and Service Providers: Ever wish you knew how competent a particular contractor or firm was before you hired them? And if you want to get into the network technician business, this chapter describes some of the hottest certifications in the industry.

Appendixes

The appendixes, with the exception of Appendix A, are all current laboratory exercises in my networking courses, developed over the years with input from other professionals in the field.

Appendix A—Network Technician's Needs: This is a listing of the tools and supplies that would be both necessary and financially feasible for a beginning network technician.

Appendix B—Visio® Technical Drawing of the LAN Lab: Microsoft Visio® is a sophisticated drawing program offering a wide range of image templates or icons that can be customized for many different industries. Visio® is currently owned by Microsoft and is compatible with all Microsoft Office products and file formats.

Appendix C—Cable Manufacture and Testing: This laboratory exercise guides students through the field manufacture of cross-connect or patch cables, cross-over cables, and a typical RJ-45 wall socket.

Appendix D—Introduction to the Fluke OneTouch Series II Network Assistant: The standard of network testers, Fluke's OneTouch® is one of the premiere testing tools on the market today. The cost of the OneTouch Series® II is typically out of reach for most technicians and/or consultants. As a marketing tool, Fluke has developed an online demonstration tool, accessible at www.fluke.com, that accurately simulates using the equipment via a standard Web browser.

Appendix E—Network Cable Verification Form: This form is a good *starting point* or template for use in an organization after either completing a network cabling installation or if you need to verify cabling that someone else has installed but there is not established documentation.

Contents of the Student CD

The student CD contains the Excel® spreadsheets for calculating budgets and bids, PowerPoint® presentations that were fictitiously given to the clients, the images in the text, and the finished BTAs.

Acknowledgments

No author can take sole credit for any academic work. I have been blessed with wonderful teachers who have challenged and inspired me. I can think back to Mrs. Norcross and Mr. Thomas at Clinton High School, who taught me to appreciate literature and translate my thoughts into words, as well as Dr. Babrakzai and Dr. Powers, who taught me logic and science at Central Missouri State University.

I have also been encouraged to higher levels of performance by colleagues and coworkers, especially during my time with SkillPath/CompuMaster Seminars and DeVRY University–Kansas City. My students have also played a part in driving my success. Without their questions and discussions, I would never have explored and refined my understanding of computing, networking, and the learning process to the extent I have today.

On a separate note, I would like to thank Dawn Daugherty, Steve Helba, Lisa Walden, and the entire staff of the Thomson Delmar Learning/ Course Technology family. For over two years Dawn quietly and patiently asked me if I had any interest in writing a textbook. Her persistence finally won me over, and I submitted a sample chapter. The result is this text.

Without the loving support of friends and family, this text would not be in your hands today. I would especially like to thank my parents, and particularly my father, who passed from us the day after I finished writing this text. Without their guidance, I would not be who I am today. To my wife and kids, thank you for the sacrifice of our family time to allow me to write when the mood struck me. This is your book as much as it is mine.

PART I

Getting Started

Laying the Foundation

1

Learning Objectives

◆ Introduce the text and become acquainted with the purpose of the text.

◆ Introduce some common-sense principles for surviving the "corporate jungle."

Why Is This Chapter Important to Me?

Although this chapter is not full of technical jargon, the information contained in it can, in many ways, determine your future success in the information technology (IT) field. Regardless of your technical prowess and expertise, soft skills (also known as *people skills*) are often more important to your economic and professional success than the ability to spout technical jargon that no one else can understand. Often it is more important to have at least a passable amount of technical information with the ability to communicate it effectively and interact with colleagues than it is to be a highly technical professional who can't communicate or interact with others.

This chapter sets the tone for the rest of the text. It is also important because it establishes a set of guidelines that are not routinely described in such a formal presentation as this text.

This text is a departure from the normal textbook with the formal writing style written in the third person. Instead the author will attempt to have a more narrative and conversational style of writing dedicated to management or business issues as opposed to the more technical information.

Introduction

It would be a technician's dream to deal only with technology! For most "techies" the ideal job would deal only with technology, the logical part of the business environment. How we could make the company's—even the world's—computers work if not for users and management edicts! But let us not forget that the users make our network necessary, and those management edicts make our network possible. With these facts in mind, let's get started.

In this text we will be designing the networks for three hypothetical companies. Although this text is not meant to replace "technology" books such as the *Network+ Guide to Networking* (Tamara Dean, Course Technologies, ISBN: 0-619-21743-X) or an equivalent text, it is meant to be used in conjunction with such books. We will focus more on management issues, network performance goals, actual network design, asset management, ease of troubleshooting, and so on.

This chapter's main goal is to effectively assess your current network assets, determine if those assets meet present management expectations, and possibly predict the future network that might match the company in the next three to five years and beyond. Although the future cannot be accurately predicted, we can still use good network management guidelines for potential future growth.

Management Guidelines

Sometimes the most difficult part of determining how to design a network is figuring out what management actually wants to do with the network and the overall organization. Some recent computer supplier commercials seem to typify the general user's inability to adequately understand and navigate the complex systems that make up the corporate network:

"Wish me luck. I'm off to crash the server."

"Have you installed that incompatible software I ordered?"

Although these are not the exact words that users and even upper management actually say, this is what we, in the IT industry, tend to hear from their statements. It is our job to reduce their frustration, minimize production losses, and offer assistance whenever problems might arise.

The main method for obtaining management's expectations of the network is to actually sit in high-level management meetings. Hearing what management wants to do with the company makes our job easier by allowing us to see "the big picture." The problem is that this picture isn't always easy to quantify or even qualify. Many executives may only have a feeling or vision about how the company will perform in the next few years. It's difficult to plan and budget based on a vague vision.

On the other hand, most techies don't know how to communicate effectively with management. If IT staff members extol the technical specifications of new hardware or software, most members of management can't understand how this will impact either the company as a whole or them in particular. What is interesting about this dilemma is that *if* the appropriate message can be sent about the cost versus the benefit, most managers can become enthusiastic about the same technology that seemed foreign and undesirable when it was presented in a different way.

Another factor when expanding an existing network (also called a *brownfield* network) as opposed to planning a new network (known as a *greenfield* network) is having a complete inventory of any network-related resources currently owned by the organization. An existing network has a whole "personality" due to the effects of myriad technologies that interact in previously unknown and unpredictable ways. It would be advisable to check with colleagues, online discussion boards, or other subject matter experts (SMEs). Often the interaction between new or upgraded technologies causes the most headaches for network engineers. It's also hard for most customers to understand if their previous versions of software worked perfectly, but the newly upgraded software doesn't seem to work as well as their previous stuff.

Professional Conduct

As a techie, it's often difficult to remember how it was when we didn't know how technology worked. Also, we're sometimes more comfortable working with technology instead of actual people. For these reasons, here are some guidelines for professional conduct:

1. Always wear professional attire. Depending on the company, this may be simple business casual or even corporate dress attire. The saying goes that "when in Rome, act like a Roman."

2. Always care about your personal hygiene. It's not uncommon to work odd or long hours, which can make regular baths, tooth brushing, and clothes changing difficult. It sounds funny, but sometimes it's a luxury to have a nice warm shower or bath. The scariest part of this guideline is that a lack of personal hygiene can sneak up on you until someone else points it out to you, making for a very awkward situation.

3. Be on time! Many people consider it extremely rude to make them wait for someone else. To some people this is even worse than having poor personal hygiene. Being late leads some to see you as unprofessional.

4. Avoid jargon as much as possible. There's nothing more frustrating than having a salesman, computer technician, doctor, lawyer, or other expert use professional jargon that the average person isn't familiar with. It is also easy to get caught up in the jargon and not be able to actually distill the complex intricacies because you've used the jargon for so long. It is embarrassing to be "called out" by a user and not be able to answer the questions in a non-technical manner.

5. Always document both the content and spirit of important meetings and all user interactions. Because most typical network personnel are incredibly overworked, they won't be able to remember exactly what happened just a few months ago. This is even more true of high-level personnel. These meetings can be touchy, especially when there is any possibility of someone not understanding exactly what was agreed upon. It's sad but true, but your notes may be needed if legal action must be taken. Notes handwritten on a legal pad or a help desk ticket will allow easier referencing of whatever has transpired in the past. It has been said that "if you can remember what you've done six months ago to a particular system, you're not doing enough."

6. Always respect both your users and your customers. In fact, many companies have begun to describe all people who use your network or its services as customers, even if they're actually internal company employees. Although they may not have the same level of expertise as the IT staff, they are still valuable employees who deserve respect and dignified treatment.

7. Keep a journal of what's been said by others, important configurations and passwords, and most important, what you've said and promised to others!

Summary

Although this is not part of the information technology industry's educational syllabus, it is vitally important to understand the interpersonal skills necessary to succeed in the IT industry. It's not only technical prowess that determines your overall success in any position or with any organization. Often it's the ability to find the technical experts or subject matter experts (SMEs) and be an effective interpreter between management and these SMEs. Also, it is quite possible to "leapfrog" over individuals with years of experience by having attained an industry-recognized certificate such as an MCSE, A+, CCNA, or the like. You can also succeed by becoming an integral part of a required business unit or by being known as the "go-to" person in the organization, even in the absence of complete mastery over a specific technology. Companies will most generally choose for advancement a dedicated, coworker-friendly individual with a good core of technical competence instead of an aloof, disinterested technical guru in a particular technology. (Such individuals often become contractors or consultants and do not enjoy employee benefits such as vacation and health care insurance.)

The author hopes the rest of this text will provide a useful framework for both the business and design of information technology and networking.

Discussion Questions

1. When starting out on a career path, it's customary (whether formally or informally) to determine what type of position you would like and its requirements. What position would you like? What are the requirements for this position?

2. Perform a cost (educational costs) versus benefit (salary) study for the top three jobs that were determined in Question 1 in your geographic region.

3. If you were hiring an IT or network technician, what would be the top five characteristics/qualities you would look for? How might that list change for an IT or network manager?

A Review of the OSI Model

2

Learning Objectives

After completing this chapter, you will be able to

- Understand the OSI model as the industry-standard convention to discuss all network communications.

- View basic network hardware in relation to the OSI model.

- Comprehend basic network communications.

Why Is This Material Important to Me?

Studying the open systems interconnect (OSI) model is not just an academic exercise. Some people assume that this "model" has no relevance to the actual consultant or practitioner. This philosophy could not be further from the truth! The OSI model was originally developed by academics to facilitate the design, manufacture, interoperability, and troubleshooting of networking between vendors or service providers.

To understand the beauty of this concept, imagine trying to communicate between two vendors such as Novell and Cisco. Invariably there will be some sort of issue with any two vendors and their products. If the actual problem was between IEEE 802.1 (a spanning tree protocol) and Novell NetWare's Internetwork Packet Exchange/Sequenced Packet Exchange (IPX/SPX) protocol suite, a technician would need to be fluent with both technologies to achieve a resolution. Otherwise, think of the hours on the phone with Cisco and Novell techs trying to translate what the other set of technicians were saying.

As an alternative, the OSI model facilitates this process by removing proprietary jargon. Instead of spending time translating each vendor's proprietary language, the process becomes much quicker and more pleasant. Spanning tree is a data link layer protocol, and Novell's IPX/SPX protocols transcend the network and transport layers. By using the OSI standard naming and concepts, both the Cisco and Novell techs can communicate and troubleshoot a problem without knowing much about either vendor's products. As an added benefit, technical sales materials are now being printed with OSI language. If salespeople can understand (or at least sell) this model, shouldn't techies be familiar with OSI?

For this text we will divide the entire telecommunications or network communications industry into two broad categories: wide area networks (WANs) and local area networks (LANs). These two broad, artificial categories allow us to divide the industry into analog and digital technologies.

WANs are a legacy of the original telephone industry, which was based on analog transmission technologies. Although we are not going to delve into the history of telecommunications, we will compare a few of its characteristics with those of LANs. For instance, telecommunications companies created their own communications standards, whether they were private organizations, pseudogovernmental groups, or complete government agencies. The industry lacked standards such as the IEEE 802.x standards for LAN technologies.

LANs were developed to connect an organization's own terminals to their mainframes or servers. As such, LANs were based on digital technologies and standards, allowing a more consistent implementation of similar technologies. This allowed the development of a standardized model for communicating between manufacturers, vendors, engineers, and consumers. The OSI model was developed and released by the International Standards Organization to provide a standardized model for use by networking professionals worldwide, regardless of their areas of expertise or company affiliation. But like other models, the OSI model is only a humanly devised method to describe network communications. After a thorough investigation of different networking technologies, the reader will find that many technologies, devices, protocols, services, and the like do not fit neatly into the finely divided layers of the OSI model.

The OSI model is divided into seven primary layers, with one of these layers being divided into two sublayers. These players are generally numbered from "bottom to top" with Layer 1 being the physical layer and Layer 7 being the application layer: hardware to software. This model is used to describe and predict the communication between two resources or nodes. Additionally, the model describes peer-to-peer communications because information added to the data stream at Layer 2 of the sending resource will be "seen" only by the Layer 2 components on the other end of the communication stream. But keep in mind that this model is just that—a model.

We will begin reviewing the OSI model by using an example of sending e-mail from a GroupWise client to an Outlook client on the other side of the continent. From the user's perspective, the process of translating actions through the OSI model is relatively transparent and straightforward. When Bob in Seattle sends e-mail using his GroupWise client to John in Maryland, who is using an Outlook client, neither user observes the mechanisms that the two systems undertake to send the mail across the Internet.

Bob in Seattle just heard a great joke from a colleague and decides to send an e-mail to John in Maryland. As Bob opens his GroupWise e-mail client, he composes the message, adds the sender information, and clicks on the send button of the GroupWise client. Then the e-mail is translated from a proprietary GroupWise format into a generic format and "chunked" into specific transmission pieces; sender and receiver information is added to the transmission pieces, and the parcel is sent through the Internet to John. John's computer takes the bits of data, strips off the sender and receiver information, takes the transmission pieces and repackages them into a whole message, and reformats the generic message into an Outlook e-mail message.

Let's break this transmission down into its constituent components by examining the communication between Bob's (sender) and John's (receiver) systems (see Table 2.1):

Sender System: Bob's System

Application Layer: Layer 7

Specific action:

> The GroupWise client is the application that takes the information Bob is typing to John. When Bob completes his e-mail message and clicks on the

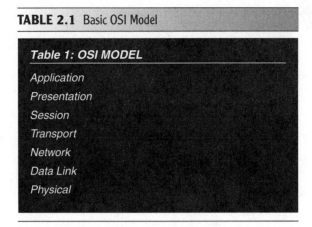

TABLE 2.1 Basic OSI Model

Table 1: OSI MODEL
Application
Presentation
Session
Transport
Network
Data Link
Physical

send button, the application layer hands the message in its proprietary format to the presentation layer for formatting.

Explanation:

In fact, any application that can be activated with a mouse click or by using a command line interface exists in Layer 7, the application layer of the OSI.

Presentation Layer: Layer 6

Specific action:

The presentation layer changes the proprietary format of the e-mail message into a generic, standards-based format that will be acceptable to any standard e-mail program.

Explanation:

The presentation layer formats proprietary data into a nonproprietary or standard data format. It also provides data encryption and data compression.

Session Layer: Layer 5

Specific action:

Bob's system makes sure that some sort of communications session has been established before attempting to send the e-mail. Without a communications session, there's no point in trying to complete the communication.

Explanation:

The session layer establishes, maintains, and terminates the communications session between two systems.

Transport Layer: Layer 4

Specific action:

After changing the GroupWise e-mail into a generic file format, the actual file is broken into data packets, labeled, and packaged for transmission.

Explanation:

The transport layer accepts the generic file from the presentation layer and divides it into the appropriate-sized parts or packets. These packets are packaged much as a printer is packaged for shipment from the manufacturer. The appropriate amount of error detection and correction mechanisms are put into the packaging; then the packets are numbered, given date and time stamps, and made ready for transmission.

Network Layer: Layer 3

Specific action:

Bob's system must know the logical or network address of John's system before the message has any chance of being delivered. At this point the physical address does not have to be known, just the logical address.

Explanation:

The logical address allows the transmission to be routed between systems, even if they physically move between locations. The logical address is like the name of the person within the mailing address of

> John Doe
> 1234 Main Street
> Anytown, MD, XXXXX-XXXX

In this case the logical address for a letter being sent to this address is "John Doe." The logical address may change: John Doe can move to another house. But the mail addressed to 1234 Main Street, the physical address, will be delivered to that location regardless of where John Doe lives.

Data Link Layer: Layer 2

Specific action:

The data link layer of Bob's system places the physical address on the data packets, now called *frames for transmission.* If both Bob's and John's systems are located on a subnet under the control of the same router, both systems would know each other's physical address.

Explanation:

There's certainly a lot going on in the data link layer. There are two specific and distinct sublayers within the data link layer. The "higher" of the two layers, the logical link control, was defined as the IEEE 802.2 standard. The "lower" of the two layers is the media access control (MAC), which defines the physical addresses of network devices known as MAC addresses.

Although there is some discrepancy about which sublayer actually contains the following functions, it is agreed that they definitely happen within the data link layer. These include the actual interaction with network device drivers and the defining of the various network standards.

Physical Layer: Layer 1

Specific actions:

Unseen to the user, the data within the frames are converted into data suitable for transmission along the media to John's computer.

Explanation:

The physical hardware devices such as the network interface cards (NICs) actually convert the digital data of 0s and 1s into digital waveforms that can be transmitted along either analog or digital transmission lines to the receiver's system.

Officially, the OSI model is composed of seven layers, which can be seen in Table 2.2 (left side). However, I've found that it's sometimes helpful to make up your own interpretation of the official model to enhance understanding. The OSI model was somewhat intimidating when I first approached it, so I developed my own model to make it less intimidating, which can be seen in Table 2.2 (right side). I grouped the physical and data link layers (Layers 1 and 2) and called them "hardware" because these components can actually be touched, felt, and installed. The application, presentation, and session layers (Layers 7, 6, and 5) were grouped together and called "software" because they are directly associated with making the communications sessions, various file formatting operations, and providing the user interface. Between the hardware and software layers, the network and transport layers (Layers 3 and 4) form the "protocols" layer (see Table 2.2).

Networking Devices

The review of the OSI model was fairly generic and without much exploration of the underlying components that make this communication possible. These underlying components form the physical and logical backbone of the network.

TABLE 2.2 Enhanced OSI Model

Table 1: OSI MODEL	
Application	
Presentation	Software
Session	
Transport	Protocols
Network	
Data Link	Hardware
Physical	

When we explored the communications between John's and Bob's computers, we started at the application layer and worked our way down. This time we'll be exploring from the bottom up because that's how your network will be physically installed.

Physical Layer: Media

The most important component of this whole network, or at least the glue that holds it together, are the networking media. Whether they are fiber optic or wireless, nothing happens without the networking media. The basic function of the physical layer is to provide electrical, optical, radio frequency, or infrared infrastructure for connecting the actual network devices.

The most widely installed, easiest to maintain, and least expensive option is copper cabling, also known as *twisted pair* because there are multiple pairs of similarly colored wires inside each cable. Cabling that is used in telecommunications and networking is constructed of several pairs of copper strands sheathed in different colored material (for identification) and twisted (to reduce cross talk between the sending and receiving wires). These have been standardized in the number and type of individual strands of wire, the gauge or diameter of the individual wires, the maximum length of cabling that can be used before signal degradation is sufficient to scramble the network communications, and the bandwidth capacity of the individual cables. The EIA/TIA committee has standardized the different types of network cabling into different categories. The most common type currently installed is Cat5e with eight wires or four pairs and a maximum of 450–500 Mbps of transmission capacity between 3 and 100 meters (8 to 328 feet). Installation of Cat5e cabling is relatively simple and inexpensive.

Fiber optic cabling does not have the electromagnetic interference or broadcasting issues of twisted pair cabling, so it's more secure. Fiber also lacks the bandwidth constraints of twisted pair. The major disadvantage is the cost of obtaining the fiber and installing it. On the upside, fiber optic cabling does not have to be upgraded whenever a new networking standard is developed; only the signaling devices on either end of the fiber need to be changed.

Wireless is a medium that is growing in popularity due to consumer demand, not because of technical capabilities. Because wireless is a broadcasting communication, the efficiency of the signaling is not nearly that of the wired media standards that are currently being installed. Additional concerns stem from lack of security and lack of overall bandwidth capacity. At present most corporate needs cannot be met by current network standards. But consumer demand and clever marketing are pushing the convenience of wireless networking.

Physical Layer: Devices

Think of a network as a set of small streams that connect into larger streams and finally into a river that connects to the ocean. In this analogy the small streams are the hubs (physical layer devices). The larger streams are the data link layer devices (bridges and switches), and the river is the network composed of network layer devices. After traveling through the physical, data link, and network layers, the systems connect with the ocean: the Internet. Using this analogy helps put into perspective the OSI network hierarchy. We will return to this model as we continue.

Besides the physical media ports and terminators, there are only two types of physical layer devices: amplifiers and repeaters.

Network amplifiers perform the same basic function as an audio amplifier. Analog or audio signals are amplified or made stronger before being transmitted down the line. The major problems with using amplifiers are twofold: (1) the noise and imperfections of the original signal are strengthened before being rebroadcast, and (2) analog signals monopolize the entire bandwidth of the communications media so that only one type of communication can occur at a time.

Network repeaters function similarly to amplifiers but for digital signals. Because digital signals are discrete values of discrete size, it is much easier to strengthen the signal without introducing noise. Any values that are outside the established values of the transmission protocol and media are dismissed. Part of the communications may have to be re-sent, but it's better to err toward caution instead of rebroadcasting an erroneous signal. A nice additional feature is the one-input-many-output feature on modern multiport repeaters, more commonly known as *hubs*.

Suppose we are discussing an eight-port hub. Whenever a transmission is sent into Port 1, the communication is broadcast through Ports 2–8. This type of communication is inefficient and has little security because every system on

that same hub receives the same information as the intended recipient. Also, all systems on the same hub share the same bandwidth in a contentious manner. Whichever system requests a bandwidth first gets the bandwidth it desires until it is finished and releases that bandwidth for others to use. If the system in Port 1 "hogs" 85 Mbps at a given time, the other systems in Ports 2–8 have to share the remaining 15 Mbps or so for the duration of the communication session. Whenever the system in Port 1 finishes its session, that bandwidth is then freed up for the others to "fight over."

Data Link Layer: Devices

As we travel up the OSI model, we stop at the data link layer, which acts as an intermediary to the physical layer and network layers. The specifics of the data link layer and its constituent sublayers are too technical for this review. But the physical address, the *MAC address*, is found in the MAC sublayer. The MAC address is important to network devices due to its "physicality." Each network device has an individual hardware number or code—its MAC address—that is permanently assigned by the manufacturer to provide verification that the network messages came from the proper source and were delivered to the proper source. (There are ways to change this address, but that discussion is outside the scope of this text.)

As described in the previous section, hubs are physical layer devices with no mechanism for addressing and no means to reduce or eliminate broadcasts or data packet collisions. Because of MAC addressing, data link layer devices can greatly reduce broadcasts and data packet collisions. Hub networks are notorious for having data packets collide due to the broadcast nature of the transmissions. As an upgrade to hubs, network engineers developed *bridges*. These bridges determine the MAC addresses of the locally attached systems and act as hubs for these devices. All other nonlocal traffic is forwarded on through the uplink port.

Although they are similar to bridges, *switches* actually form an on-demand circuit between sender and receiver systems. The major difference between bridges and switches is that switches, because they form on-demand circuits, do not share bandwidth and effectively multiply the usable bandwidth instead of having to share it between systems. As you might expect, no company even manufactures or installs bridges any longer. In fact, almost the entire industry has changed over from hubs and bridges to switches.

A *collision domain* is the totality of all physical devices connected by physical layer devices such as hubs. This means that all devices that are connected "beneath" a data link device, such as a bridge or switch, share a common bandwidth space where all packets from these systems can collide and become unusable. As a general rule, large collision domains have a negative effect on overall network performance. The smaller the collision domain is, the less likely there will be a collision. Adding bridges and switches breaks up the size of a collision domain or, said another way, creates segmentation within the network. Think of the collision domain as an individual stream before it joins another larger stream, with all the water able to mingle. Any pollution or murkiness can affect all the other water in that part of the stream. By adding dams along the stream, the different portions of the stream remain relatively unaffected by the other portions of the stream.

Network Layer Devices

Until now we have had only physical locations and hardware addresses to designate and control how things in our network function and communicate. Now we have network or logical addresses to help determine how our network will function. At this level we have such things as IP addresses. Because these are globally unique and assigned by a network administrator and therefore not "locked" into a particular location, network administrators have added flexibility in designing their networks. This also adds to the possible complexity and potential troubles of the resulting network. Engineers realized that the existing networking devices would not work; something new had to be developed to help facilitate this.

The new device is called a *router*. The first routers were actually computers with two or more network interfaces. Any system with more than one network interface is said to be *multi-homed*. Even the newest, most feature-laden routers from companies such as Cisco, Bay Networks, Nortel, and others are still basically computers with multiple network interfaces that transfer packets between networks. Without some sort of automatic configuration mechanism, a multiple-router network could quickly become unwieldy. Routing algorithms or protocols were created to facilitate the "auto discovery" and configuration of the router infrastructure. This helps eliminate human entry errors and allows larger, more complex networks. Routers can also be seen as "gatekeepers" between networks. Routers make the modern age of the Internet possible.

Additional Non-OSI Model Devices

Although they are not specifically part of the OSI, some devices help us enhance our network experience and manage our networks more professionally. Devices such as Apache Web server software do not easily fit into the OSI. The Web server unquestionably uses the OSI to communicate with its clients, but it exists outside the OSI model.

One such device is a *firewall*; but to understand this device, we'll have to consider building and construction. If you can imagine a strip mall or other multi-unit structure, visualize walls that extend up through the ceiling to separate different parts of the building so that fire cannot spread easily from one unit to another. Think of these walls as a mechanism to minimize the spread of fire, noise, biohazards, or the like between the units (or subnets) within the overall structure (or network). Firewalls, whether software or hardware or a combination of the two, are used to selectively allow certain packets to enter and exit a network. They can effectively "hide" your network behind a strong network security countermeasure. Developed in the 1980s by Marcus J. Ranum (www.ranum.com), firewalls have become an essential part of network security.

A second device is a *proxy server*. Internet requests are made to an existing Web site from a system. Instead of the system communicating to the remote Web site, the system asks the proxy server to get the information for it. The proxy server retrieves the requested information from the remote Web site and makes a copy of it on the local proxy server's hard drive for the original system to access. Thus the original system never actually comes into contact with the remote, and presumably insecure, Web server.

The last device we'll discuss in this chapter is a *gateway*. A gateway device is a network protocol translator. If one segment of the network uses TCP/IP as its communications protocol and the other segments use IPX/SPX, an engineer will need to install a protocol gateway to translate and provide communications between the two disparate network protocols.

The term *gateway* has been used in at least a couple of different contexts. Of course we have the computer and electronics manufacturer Gateway with the familiar "cow print" logos and graphics. There is also a gateway that provides protocol translation such as between IPX/SPX and TCP/IP. It is necessary with this type of gateway to have multiple NICs installed (called multi-homed) with *all* of the needed protocols installed as well, as described in the text. Another type of gateway is an IP gateway such as is needed to communicate from the local network and an external network. Actually, this type of gateway can be viewed as a subset of the gateway discussed in the body of the text.

Summary

We have reviewed the OSI model not only as a method to communicate about using a network but also as a language to provide commonality between different manufacturers and engineers. It is often useful to consider a familiar analogy such as a letter being addressed and sent through the postal service. This helps to relate unfamiliar or difficult subjects such as the OSI model. The OSI allows the products of different organizations, standards bodies, and manufacturers to interoperate with a universal language.

The seven layers of the OSI model can be grouped into three main divisions. The lower layers (physical and data link) can be categorized as hardware or more physically based. The middle layers (network and transport) are where the majority of the protocol activity is located. The upper layers (session, presentation, and application) are where the actual communication between end user systems occurs. These provide the functionality that allows communication with e-mail servers, Web servers, file sharing, and so on.

Discussion Questions

1. John is a network technician at a large accounting firm. A user on the fourth floor calls him because she can't connect to the Internet. Using the OSI as a guide, provide John with a step-by-step process to determine what the user's issues are.

2. In a nontechnical example, use the OSI as a guide to describe how that process works. Sending a letter to a prospective employer or manufacturing and shipping a printer from a factory to a retail outlet are good examples to use as a starting point. Don't worry if your example doesn't use every layer of the OSI; remember, this is only an exercise to become more familiar with the OSI.

3. Pick up a computer or network catalog from any regional or national vendor. Count the number of times the OSI model layers are used to describe the networking devices. Also note the different types of products that are described using OSI nomenclature.

3

Network Basics

Learning Objectives

After reading this chapter, you will be able to

- ◆ Compare and contrast the costs and benefits of the different networking media.

- ◆ Compare and contrast different networking devices and their functions.

- ◆ Describe the functions of different networking devices as compared with the OSI model.

- ◆ Describe the overall flow of data across a network based on the network architectures.

Why Is This Material Important to Me?

This chapter lays the practical foundation for the fundamental understanding of the overall network and its components. Some of the explanations of the different components are somewhat oversimplified here. For example, certain manufacturers have developed routing switches. As far as this course is concerned, such a hybrid device does not exist because a router routes packets and a switch makes an on-demand circuit. After the basic concepts are clearly understood, we can look more deeply at them and explore hybrid devices.

OSI Model Summary

As a quick summary of the OSI model from the last chapter, network professionals have divided the process of sending data communications between two nodes into seven distinct layers. These layers are mostly independent of each other, with the products from the processes in one layer being handed to the next layer, either up or down the OSI (only one way at a time). Because of the layered or stratified characteristics of the OSI, it makes products (either hardware or software) easier to manufacture, cheaper to purchase, and interoperable between vendors.

This chapter should give you the practical application and examples for a more concrete understanding. Those of you with many years of experience or perhaps a networking certificate may want to skim the next section.

Basic Terminology

Circuit	A circuit, in its simplest form, is a metal wire (almost always copper) that is connected to both the "+" or positive side of a power source and the "−" or negative side of the same power source. This allows energy to flow from the positive end of the power source and into the negative end of the power source. If there is a break in the circuit, the circuit has a "short" in it. This is important to networking because if a resource has no connection to the network, no communications will be sent. All network traffic is sent through electrical pulses (through copper), through light waves or pulses (through fiber optic lines), or through some sort of wireless transmission (through the air).
Bandwidth	The collection or sum of frequencies that can be transmitted across a particular medium is called *bandwidth* (BW). This is typically measured in bits per second units such as 100 Mbps. A higher BW can transmit more data at a time. The deceptive thing is that transmission speed is not affected by higher BW.

	However, the overall time it takes for a particular download is shortened by higher BW. Think of higher BW transmissions as having more "pipes" to speed the packets to their destination.
Network	A network is a collection of resources connected together to facilitate the sharing of those resources between the users or devices on the network. Networks can be composed of PCs, servers, printers, Web sites, and so on.
Cross talk	Cross talk is the phenomenon experienced when data cables are installed near other cables transmitting electricity. This can harm network throughput. It's not uncommon to experience intermittent but persistent communication errors when a data cable has been installed too close to an electrical wire or fixture, such as a fluorescent light fixture.
Protocol	Software that exist as a liaison between the network devices and the operating system are called *protocols*. Another way of looking at protocols is that they are the language for communicating across a network between different devices.

Network Cabling, Media, and So On: Layer 1

Network media are the materials via which data are actually sent throughout the network. (Many of these terms can be used in different contexts, but here they will be defined with a telecommunications/networking slant.) Network media are generally divided into three distinct types: copper cabling (coaxial and twisted pair); fiber optic; and wireless media. Each of these has its own strengths and weaknesses due to various characteristics and would be appropriate for the right network or network segment.

Copper cabling has been around for over 100 years and has been the staple for both analog and digital transmissions since that time. Because of the metallic nature of the conductor, installation is relatively easy (either in a field location or inside a building) and durable. Although there are metals with better conductivity such as silver, gold, and platinum, these materials are more expensive and hence undesirable for these uses. In fact, the author knows of an installation of two-wire telephone cable (complete with 100-year-old utility poles) that was in continuous use until the mid-1900s. Regardless of its historical significance, solid copper core cabling is not installed in a contemporary network except in coaxial cables. Current copper cables can be divided into two distinct types: coaxial cable, such as in cable TV installations, and twisted pair cabling, such as standard telephone or network installations.

Coaxial cabling or coax (see Figure 3.1) is manufactured with a central core composed of a solid copper wire surrounded by a dielectric insulator. This is encased in a foil shield and/or a metallic braided sheath or sleeve. The entire cable is then enclosed with a tough rubbery coating, making it extremely strong

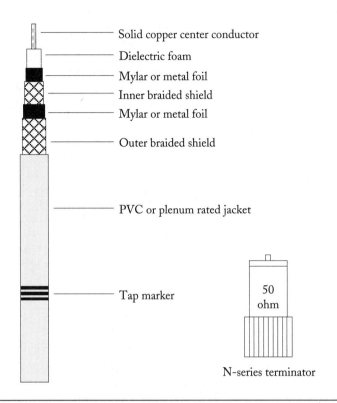

Solid copper center conductor

Dielectric foam

Mylar or metal foil

Inner braided shield

Mylar or metal foil

Outer braided shield

PVC or plenum rated jacket

Tap marker

50 ohm

N-series terminator

FIGURE 3.1 ◆ Coaxial Cable (Cutaway View)

and weather-resistant. Because of the construction with the various metallic layers, the overall cable strength is exceptional, and it possesses a high degree of immunity to interference. Unfortunately, the advantages of coaxial cabling have not kept it from obsolescence. Its major restriction is a limited amount of BW. Coax cabling is just too bulky and costly for the BW it provides, making it suitable only for use as a backbone segment between buildings, different floors, and in similar settings. In all fairness, there are several high-bandwidth coax standards, but most of the industry has turned toward twisted pair as a better alternative.

Twisted pair (TP) (see Figure 3.2) is made up of smaller and separate pairs of wires (one for sending and one for receiving). The two wires of the pair are twisted along its length to minimize cross talk between the pairs, yielding higher BWs than are possible with standard coax. Although not as rugged in construction, TP is cheaper and easier to install in less than ideal environments. The different types of TP cabling are divided into categories (see Figure 3.3),

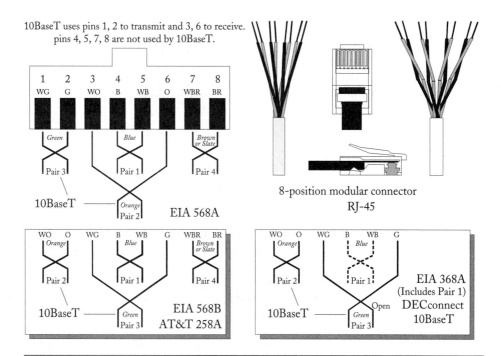

10BaseT uses pins 1, 2 to transmit and 3, 6 to receive. pins 4, 5, 7, 8 are not used by 10BaseT.

8-position modular connector RJ-45

FIGURE 3.2 ◆ Twisted Pair Cable: Cat5 or Cat5e (Cutaway View)

Cable Category	Data Rate	Bandwidth	Application
Category 1 (CAT1)	20 Kbps		Analog voice, doorbell wiring
Category 2 (CAT2)	4 Mbps	1 MHz	Voice
Category 3 (CAT3)	10 Mbps	16 MHz	Voice and data on 10BaseT Ethernet
Category 4 (CAT4)	16 Mbps	20 MHz	Token Ring and 10BaseT Ethernet
Category 5 (CAT5)	100 Mbps	100 MHz	100BaseT Ethernet, 10BaseT Ethernet, ATM
Enhanced CAT5	1.2 Gbps	200 MHz	Same as CAT5, Gigabit Ethernet
Category 6 (CAT6)	2.4 Gbps	250 MHz	Same as Enhanced CAT5, but better performance
Category 7 (CAT7)	Unknown at this time	600 MHz	Same as Enhanced CAT5; standard was still in testing at press time

FIGURE 3.3 ◆ Twisted Pair Wiring Categories

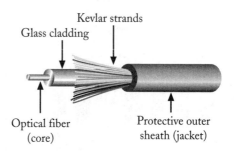

Glass cladding
Kevlar strands
Optical fiber (core)
Protective outer sheath (jacket)

FIGURE 3.4 ◆ Fiber Optic

each with its own AWG conductor standard, physical limitations, and maximum BW. The current standard of choice for LANs is Category 5 Enhanced or Cat5e. Cat5e is essentially the same as Cat5, except the gluing of the wire pairs together increases the maximum BW from 100 Mbps to 450 or more Mbps. Despite its advantages, it is typically not immune to broadcasting and interference unless specially shielded twisted pair (STP) wiring is installed properly.

Fiber optic cabling (see Figure 3.4) is the data standard of the present and the future. Data are transmitted through the fiber using either LED pulses or different wavelengths of light along its glass or plastic "conductor." Because the conductor is made of extremely fragile material, it is harder to install than TP (although it's almost as easy to terminate fiber as it is to terminate TP) and must be carefully protected from damage. It's also more costly—almost four or five times more expensive than TP—but the BW alone is worth it. Imagine having a cable plant that doesn't need to be upgraded in the foreseeable future. When new innovations arrive, the signaling devices (and possibly the terminators) can simply be installed, and the existing fiber will be able to handle it with ease! An additional advantage is that fiber is immune to electronic eavesdropping and interference, making it a better choice for highly sensitive or electrically noisy installations.

The last medium we will discuss is wireless (see Figure 3.5). Wireless media are disparate technologies that use microwave, laser, infrared, or radio frequency signals. The main lure of wireless is the convenience of not having wires to "tie you down." Additionally, the cost has plummeted over the past few years. The major disadvantage is the almost complete lack of security. This statement is in direct contradiction to claims from many manufacturers, who say that their messages are convenient and secure. By their nature, wireless systems are inherently insecure because some sort of signal is being sent through the air to a system removed from the sender. The only signals that

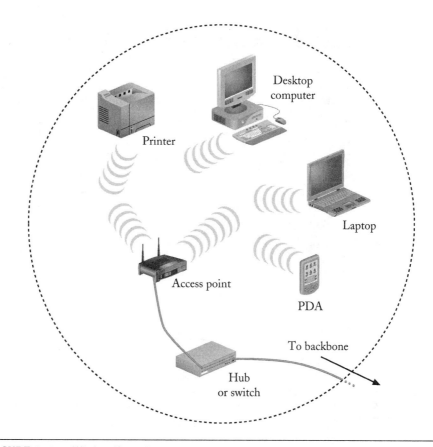

FIGURE 3.5 ◆ Wireless Network

have passed the scrutiny of network security experts are those being developed and purchased by the military and direct communication with satellites orbiting the planet, usually connecting to a WAN of some form. Consumer or business-grade products do not have the same level of security as these military devices. Organizations desiring wireless networking should weigh the costs of losing confidential information (loss of consumer confidence, loss of a competitive edge, the expense of possible litigation) against the possible benefits of convenience and worker and customer satisfaction. These may be acceptable risks within certain portions of a network for specific reasons, but it is not recommended that large portions of a network be wireless.

Cable Type	Cost	Installation	Capacity	Range	EMI/RFI
Coaxial ThinNet	Less than STP	Easy and relatively inexpensive	10 Mbps typical	185 m	Less sensitive than UTP
Coaxial ThickNet	More than STP, less than fiber	Easy	10 Mbps typical	500 m	Less sensitive than UTP
STP	More than UTP, less than ThickNet	Fairly easy	16 Mbps typical, up to 500 Mbps	100 m	Less sensitive than UTP
UTP	Lowest	Easy and relatively inexpensive	10 Mbps typical, up to 4.8 Gbps	100 m	Most sensitive
Fiber optic	Among the highest; differs by application	Expensive and difficult	100 Mbps to 200 Gbps	2000 to 3000 km	Insensitive

FIGURE 3.6 ◆ Network Media Comparisons Chart

A thorough treatment of the different types of network media is beyond the scope of this text, but some understanding can be gleaned from Figure 3.6. Typically the more the network media costs, the more bandwidth is available and the longer the media will be viable within a network infrastructure. But this is only a *rule of thumb*—not a statement that can be used to justify the cost of your next network cabling project!

Amplifiers and Repeaters: Layer 1

The other components are the termination components or signal regenerators of the physical layer. These are in the form of the cable terminators (see Figure 3.7), face plates, junction boxes, cable raceways, ladder racks, patch panels, and so on (see Figure 3.8). Additionally, a network (unless it's composed of only two resources) must have some sort of signal regeneration device. Analog signals, such as voice communications, are regenerated using an amplifier, which makes the waveforms stronger but also strengthens any noise. Digital signals, such as data communications, are regenerated using a repeater. Repeaters are somewhat different due to the nature of digital signals. Digital signals, unlike analog waveforms, consist of a discrete or expected range. Because the signals are composed of discrete units, if a signal received from the sending system is outside the specified norm, the signal is rejected.

Specification	Male Connector (front view)	Male Connector (side view)	Female Receptacle (front view)	Application
AUI (DB-15)			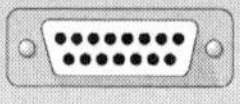	Used on coaxial cabling for Thicknet (10Base5 Ethernet).
N-series connector		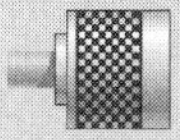		Used on coaxial cabling for Thicknet (10Base5 Ethernet) networks.
BNC				Used on coaxial cabling for Thinnet (10Base2 Ethernet) networks.
Type 1 IBM data connector			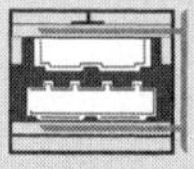	Used on older token ring networks; has been replaced by RJ-45 connectors on newer token ring networks.
DB-9				Used on older token ring networks; has been replaced by RJ-45 connectors on newer token ring networks.
RJ-11			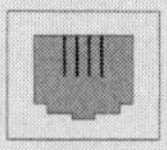	Used on twisted pair cabling for telephone systems (and some older twisted pair networks).
RJ-45				Used on twisted pair cabling for modern networks.
ST				Used on fiber optic cabling (for example, on 10BaseF or 100BaseF networks).
SC				Used on fiber optic cabling (for example, 10BaseF or 100BaseF networks).
USB	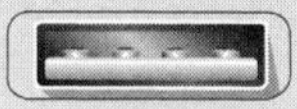	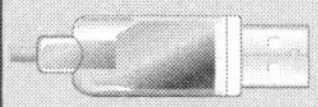		Used to connect external peripherals such as modems, mice, audio players, and NICs.

FIGURE 3.7 ◆ Various Network Terminators

A special type of repeater is the multiport repeater or hub (see Figure 3.9). A hub is a Layer 1 device that repeats the network signal received from one port throughout the other ports. The signal is regenerated (or brought back up to the intended strength) and then distributed to the other systems. The addition of a network hub allows the signal to be sent further, aids in the addition of other devices by having multiple ports for multiple devices, and helps add fault tolerance to the network in case of network failure. The only disadvantage in adding hubs to a network is that all the systems connected to the hub share the same bandwidth.

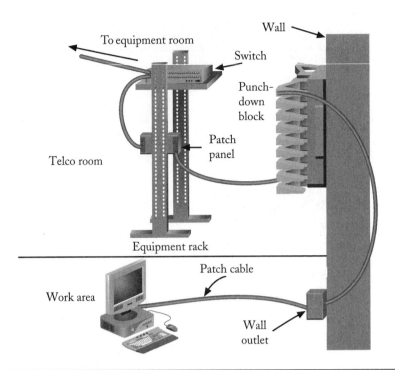

FIGURE 3.8 ◆ Typical UTP Cabling Installation

FIGURE 3.9 ◆ Hubs

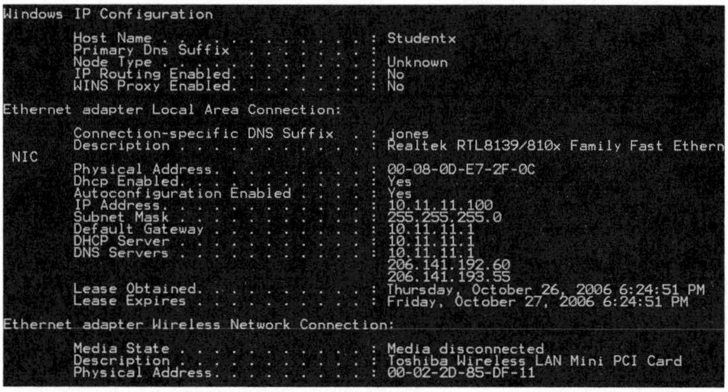

```
Windows IP Configuration

        Host Name . . . . . . . . . . . . . : Studentx
        Primary Dns Suffix . . . . . . . . :
        Node Type . . . . . . . . . . . . . : Unknown
        IP Routing Enabled. . . . . . . . . : No
        WINS Proxy Enabled. . . . . . . . . : No

Ethernet adapter Local Area Connection:

        Connection-specific DNS Suffix  . : jones
        Description . . . . . . . . . . . . : Realtek RTL8139/810x Family Fast Ethern
NIC
        Physical Address. . . . . . . . . . : 00-08-0D-E7-2F-0C
        Dhcp Enabled. . . . . . . . . . . . : Yes
        Autoconfiguration Enabled . . . . : Yes
        IP Address. . . . . . . . . . . . . : 10.11.11.100
        Subnet Mask . . . . . . . . . . . . : 255.255.255.0
        Default Gateway . . . . . . . . . . : 10.11.11.1
        DHCP Server . . . . . . . . . . . . : 10.11.11.1
        DNS Servers . . . . . . . . . . . . : 10.11.11.1
                                              206.141.192.60
                                              206.141.193.55
        Lease Obtained. . . . . . . . . . . : Thursday, October 26, 2006 6:24:51 PM
        Lease Expires . . . . . . . . . . . : Friday, October 27, 2006 6:24:51 PM

Ethernet adapter Wireless Network Connection:

        Media State . . . . . . . . . . . . : Media disconnected
        Description . . . . . . . . . . . . : Toshiba Wireless LAN Mini PCI Card
        Physical Address. . . . . . . . . . : 00-02-2D-85-DF-11
```

FIGURE 3.10 ◆ MAC Address

MAC Addresses: Layer 2

The data link layer is actually composed of two sublayers: the media access control or MAC and the logical link control (LLC). The MAC layer governs how network devices will communicate with the actual network media. There are a few stipulations before the MAC allows devices to access the network media. One is that each device has a specific and unique address. This hardware address (see Figure 3.10), as the "physical address," is one way the network knows which device to deliver its data to. Without a physical address encoded into the actual network interface, everyone would receive the data transmissions destined for a single recipient.

Think of the MAC as the address of your house. Whether or not you move, the house address stays the same. (Of course this doesn't apply to historic houses that have to be moved in the name of "progress" or historic preservation.) This will be contrasted to the logical address in Layer 3.

Bridges and Switches: Layer 2

As an upgrade to the capabilities of the network hub, the network bridge has the same repeating capabilities with the added functionality of being able to identify those systems directly connected to it using the MAC address. This helps to segment the network so that only the traffic that is not local gets broadcast through the uplink port. All other local traffic is kept within the LAN and not sent forth. For their time, bridges were a major upgrade in network performance; but they have been superseded by better technologies such as switches.

FIGURE 3.11 ◆ Switches

Switches (see Figure 3.11) follow a parallel method of network communication distribution. Switches, reading the local MAC addresses, are able to make an on-demand circuit between the sending and receiving ports. So much better is their performance that switches, on a practical level, don't share bandwidth as a hub or bridge must do. If four systems were connected to a 100 Mbps hub, *all* systems would have to share that 100 Mbps of bandwidth. With a comparable switch, each system that was transmitting would effectively have 100 Mbps. This multiplies the available bandwidth that the entire network possesses. Switches are the current state-of-the-art devices for LAN communications.

> Switches don't really multiply the available bandwidth within a network. On a practical level, the user feels that there is an unshared amount of bandwidth available only for his or her use. In actuality, there is some latency due to the establishing of a session, sending the communication, and then terminating the session. The user cannot detect such latency, but it can be seen in careful monitoring by a packet analyzer.

LLC: Layer 2

Although some people disagree with the presentation here, the standard LAN architectures and OS drivers exist in the LLC. This allows the information at the MAC sublayer to communicate with the components of the network layer, making the LLC a liaison between the MAC and network layers. Additionally, the LLC is where the drivers are loaded to translate between the operating system and the network components.

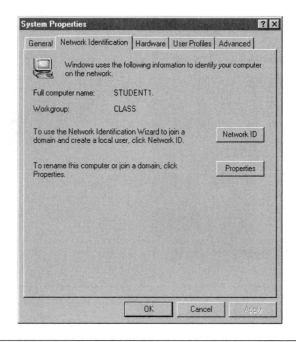

FIGURE 3.12 ◆ NetBEUI Address

Network Addressing: Layer 3

Remember that the MAC address is the physical address assigned to a network interface (like a house address). The network address is the address that is given to it but that must be of the same type as the network protocol (like the occupants of the house). For instance, a network that is using TCP/IP would have network addresses in the form of 10.9.9.6. It would not be useful to have a NetBEUI address, such as "jmiers" (see Figure 3.12). These network addresses are assigned by the network administrator, unlike the MAC address.

Routers and Switches: Layer 3

With the advent of network addresses, bridges have become less of an answer for network engineers. Switches offered a better solution but also had limitations of size and addressing. When networks became too large, switches were not able to effectively handle the network traffic. One upgrade that has attempted to rectify this inadequacy is the advent of network switching based

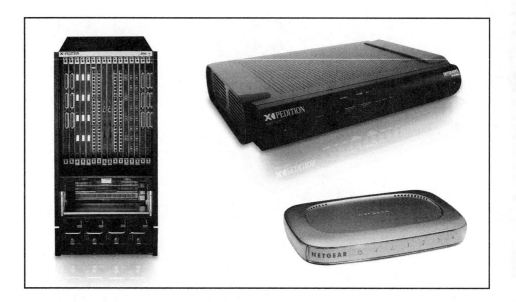

FIGURE 3.13 ◆ Routers

on network addressing. This type of addressing makes network transmission much faster and more efficient. But even with this type of switching, the network cannot react to changing network conditions with much of an interactive solution. Switches do not have the capability to determine the best path to a particular segment on the network. They can only send the data packets where the switch has been programmed to send them. If there is a problem with that link, the switch cannot determine a different path to bypass the problem.

As an alternative, routers *can* determine the most appropriate path through the network. In their simplest form, routers are devices that have multiple network interfaces (one interface for each distinct network with which they will be communicating) and the ability to transfer packets of information between these networks (called *routing*). The earliest routers were computers running UNIX or other OS with multiple NICs. The original design has been improved upon by such companies as Cisco, Nortel, Big Iron, and others. Now residential broadband routers are small, relatively inexpensive, fairly easy to install and configure, and available at local retail stores. Of course, large corporations still require specialized routers (see Figure 3.13) that have grown much more complex, are programmed to provide a wider range of applications, and have greatly increased in price since their early days.

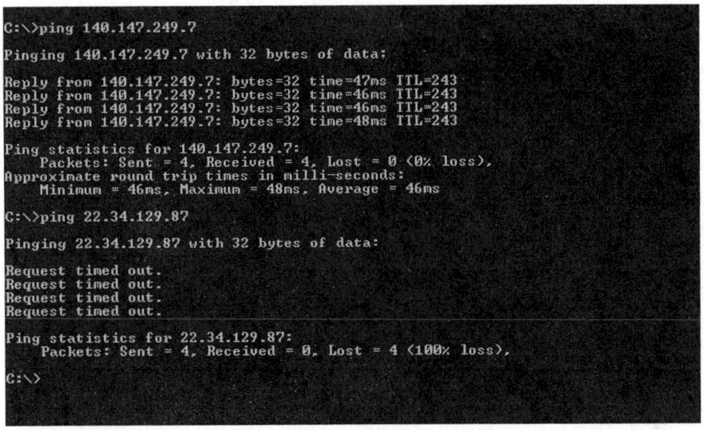

```
C:\>ping 140.147.249.7

Pinging 140.147.249.7 with 32 bytes of data:

Reply from 140.147.249.7: bytes=32 time=47ms TTL=243
Reply from 140.147.249.7: bytes=32 time=46ms TTL=243
Reply from 140.147.249.7: bytes=32 time=46ms TTL=243
Reply from 140.147.249.7: bytes=32 time=48ms TTL=243

Ping statistics for 140.147.249.7:
    Packets: Sent = 4, Received = 4, Lost = 0 (0% loss),
Approximate round trip times in milli-seconds:
    Minimum = 46ms, Maximum = 48ms, Average = 46ms

C:\>ping 22.34.129.87

Pinging 22.34.129.87 with 32 bytes of data:

Request timed out.
Request timed out.
Request timed out.
Request timed out.

Ping statistics for 22.34.129.87:
    Packets: Sent = 4, Received = 0, Lost = 4 (100% loss),

C:\>
```

FIGURE 3.14 ◆ Pinging a Web Site to Show the Router Network

Routers are necessary to connect different networks together. Without routers, networks just become larger and larger entities with few "borders." Routers serve as borders between networks of different departments within a company, between companies, and even between countries. This is accomplished with the use of routing protocols. *Routing protocols* are used between routers to determine the most efficient paths through the networks. Remember, the route with the fewest links is not always the most efficient due to network outages, faster but more numerous links, and broken links. Routers "talk" to one another about the condition and specifications of their network interfaces. If there is a break in the link between two switches, the switches continue to try to communicate with each other until either the problem is resolved or they are reset by a network engineer. Routers can determine which segment is broken and then redirect their communications around the problems so that the data transmissions are actually delivered to the correct recipients.

This capability allows such applications as the Internet. One way to see the routing network behind network transmissions is to use a command prompt or DOS command called "ping." The command's syntax goes something like this: "ping 127.0.0.1". Ping sends a specific request for communication through the network to determine if a particular network resource is available. If establishing communication is not enough, you can invoke a more robust version of the ping command by using a program called "tracert." By performing a "tracert" to a remote location, you can see the complex network that is traveled by each individual packet from here to there (see Figure 3.14). In fact, this routing network can change based on network usage, upgraded equipment, broken segments, and the like. With a switched network, the user would not know why a particular Web site could not be reached. The transmission simply wouldn't go through.

Layers 4 through 7

Except for a few exceptions such as Layer 4 switches, no other devices exist in these layers of the OSI model. Certainly there are protocols and applications that exist and provide services and functionalities to the network; but no devices in these layers will be discussed in this text.

Network Architectures

Although a network installation tech can succeed without delving into the depths of network architectures, it is helpful to understand how information flows from one side of the network to another. Four basic types of architectures are used in local area networking today. Their complexities are beyond the scope of this text, but we'll dig in just a bit.

The first architecture is a bus (see Figure 3.15). A bus is a single communication channel connecting multiple systems with a terminator attached to

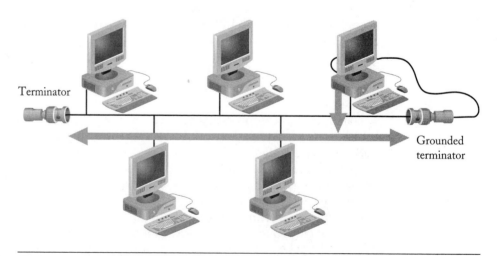

FIGURE 3.15 ◆ Bus Network

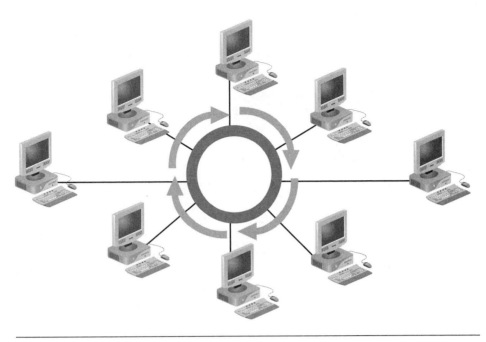

FIGURE 3.16 ◆ Ring Network

each end. Although this is an easy network to set up and understand, it also has the lowest available bandwidth and the lowest reliability. To much the same effect, a ring (see Figure 3.16) is a reconfigured bus whose ends are connected together.

The star architecture (see Figure 3.17) is the most popular and cost-effective network architecture. Stars give each system its own connection to a centralized communications device, generically called a *hub*. There are several benefits to this architecture. First, each system has its own bus connection to the hub, which allows more usable bandwidth to each device on the network. Second, because each system is hooked directly into a hub, the downing of one system doesn't disrupt the rest as in a bus or ring network. Third, multiple buses can be hooked together into large, intricate networks.

The last basic architecture is a mesh system (see Figure 3.18). A mesh can be thought of as multiple star networks hooked together with redundant links. Although it is much more expensive, a mesh is *the* must for organizations that require absolute uptime. Multiple outages can happen simultaneously with few ill effects to overall network performance. Of course, overall performance is degraded by the amount of bandwidth being routed to fewer channels, but the network remains up and running.

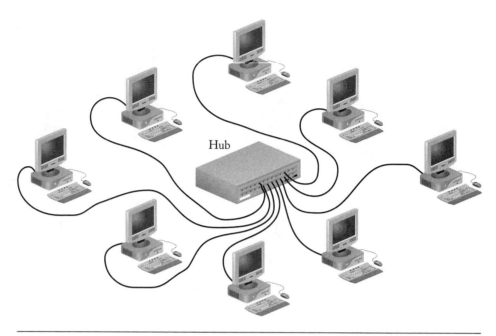

FIGURE 3.17 ◆ Star Network

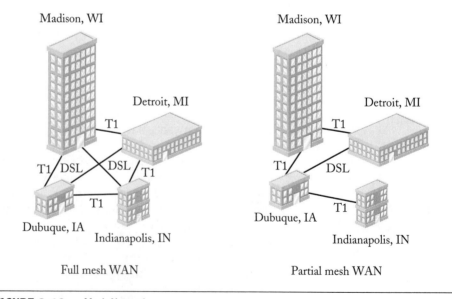

FIGURE 3.18 ◆ Mesh Network

Summary

This chapter reinforced the OSI model by exploring the different physical components of a network. These can be summarized as follows:

Layer 1	Physical media = copper, twisted pair, fiber optic, wireless. Physical devices = amplifiers (used for analog) and repeaters/hubs (used for digital).
Layer 2	Physical address = MAC address. Physical devices = bridges (improved hubs) and switches (on-demand circuits).
Layer 3	Logical addresses = protocol addresses such as IP, IPX/SPX, AppleTalk, and the like. Physical devices = routers (connecting two or more networks) and switches (on-demand circuits).
Layers 4–7	There are no devices that this book will cover.

We also explored network architectures to show how data flow from one side of a network to the other. The basic types are bus, ring, star, and mesh. Remember that the bus and ring are basically the same architecture with the same pros and cons. The star and mesh are multiple-bus architectures with added redundancy and fault tolerance capabilities.

Discussion Questions

1. Contact the IT staff at your school or work environment and ask them for a tour of the network or a diagram of the network architecture.

2. Obtain a network catalog or visit the Web site of a nationally recognized sales organization. Obtain specifications (cost, number of ports, how many can be connected together, latency, overall throughput) for the following devices:

   a. Layer 1 hub (unmanaged).

   b. Layer 1 hub (managed).

   c. Layer 2 switch.

   d. Layer 3 switch.

   e. Residential broadband router.

   f. SOHO router.

   g. Enterprise-grade router.

3. After researching the devices in Question 2, which would you use in the following networks?

   a. Three computers in a home with digital cable access.

   b. A small (five computers or so) professional office.

   c. A branch office in a professional building with 25 computers.

4

Asset Management

Learning Objectives

After reading this chapter, you will be able to

- Accurately ascertain what equipment is currently installed or associated with the existing network.

- Justify what is on the network and why more (or different) components need to be purchased and installed.

- "Hand off" the computer-related assets to the accounting department or other interested parties.

- Justify the cost and lost productivity associated with performing a physical inventory or an automated inventory.

Why Is This Material Important to Me?

Imagine this nightmarish scenario after a network breach: You as the IT manager are called into an emergency meeting of the board of directors. Officially they want to ask only a few friendly questions, but you have your suspicions! After you are seated and pleasantries are exchanged, you are asked for a recap of the situation as it is currently known. You relate that a network security breach was detected over the weekend from inside the company's network. It is uncertain how this occurred, and you assure the board that everything within your power is being done to find the leak and plug it.

They nod in agreement, wanting more specifics but understanding that there are none. One board member, Mr. Smithson, has a question. He's been against all this "high-tech mumbo-jumbo" from the start. "If you're doing so well as IT manager and we've spent all of these vast sums of money on network security, how is it that a security breach occurred and you have no concrete answers?" How will you answer these questions?

Another situation that sends chills through the IT department is a physical audit that shows a discrepancy between what should exist but is nowhere to be found. It's not uncommon for a large organization, university, or government agency to conduct a physical audit (also known as asset management or physical inventory plus the accounting documents of what should be there) and find that cars, computers, tools, or the like are missing. Image the embarrassment and loss of credibility for the operations manager (or whoever is ultimately responsible) once these facts are made known by an ambitious insider who's trying to climb the corporate ladder at your expense.

This chapter introduces some of these seemingly peripheral topics to the network designer, but it really is indispensable to determining how much equipment is currently associated with the network. Without knowing what is currently installed, it will be much more difficult to plan the network and its further growth. The principles in this chapter don't usually become important until after some sort of natural disaster, network catastrophe, security breach, or denial of a proposed budget.

Accounting Documents

Any organization of a size that needs a network enough to bring in an outside consultant will have a well-defined accounting system and probably a good set of documents showing when those items were purchased. These may be receipts, e-mail confirmations from vendors, account numbers and registrations so that purchases can be investigated by the vendors, or the like. Some organizations are quite organized and will have these readily available; others will be organized but will be reluctant to grant the clearance for viewing such documents. Still other firms will have no idea what you are asking for but would be willing to provide the documents if they could be found, and some organizations will have no idea what you are asking for and will be unwilling to provide any assistance in procuring any of this information. Although there are no official statistics about the percentage of organizations that fall within each of these groups, the author suspects that most organizations are in the "you-can-have-them-if-we-could-find-them" group.

These documents are useful for determining the actual network inventory, and there are several other reasons to have these documents on hand:

1. Knowing what is already purchased reduces or eliminates duplication.

2. Having several years' worth of these data can help you estimate how much the company has historically spent on its IT budget.

3. It's easier to record inventory when it comes in rather than after it has been put into production.

4. With the vast number of illegally installed software copies on the rise, software publishers are likely to conduct software audits of their customers. If this becomes more common, the cost of litigation will far outweigh almost any sort of labor needed to obtain an accurate inventory.

Physical Inventory/Audit

If you cannot find a complete set of accounting documents, you're going to have to do the hard work yourself. The task that most taxes the patience of most IT personnel is performing a physical inventory of all network-related equipment. This includes but is not limited to user workstations, servers, hubs, switches, routers, and so on. The cost of peripheral cards or modules may be much more than the base hardware. And an often overlooked component in a physical inventory is the software that has been installed on systems attached to the network. For an example, the cost of the hardware to build a personal computer may be as little a few hundred dollars. That cost can rise to several hundred or even a few thousand dollars after the purchase of the operating system, productivity software, any custom published software necessary for organization-specific tasks, utility software, and the like.

Actually sending a technician to every user's desk and taking inventory of the associated hardware and software can be a daunting and very time-consuming task. Let's do some rough calculations of the cost of performing a physical inventory. Although these figures are hypothetical, they provide some rough estimates of the cost:

Average hourly rate of PC/IT technician	*= $15*
Average time for a PC to reboot	*= 10 minutes*
Average time for a technician to log hardware information (Windows)	*= 30 minutes*
Average time for a technician to obtain software registration numbers	*= 30–60 minutes*
Labor cost per PC	*= $17.50–25.00*

A network of 10 computers doesn't have a huge direct cost associated with the inventory—around $200. But another cost is any lost productivity associated with the inventory, which typically equals that of the inventory itself. In our 10-computer network the inventory can thus cost up to $500.

In a company with 25 computers the costs and the lost productivity of the technicians increase by more than a factor of 2.5. Now the direct inventory cost approaches $1,250 or so, with lost productivity at least equal to that amount.

Let's take this to a higher level: 500 computers. The costs are staggering! It would take technicians at least 833 hours at a cost of $12,500 (plus the lost productivity). Of course there must be a better solution.

Automatic Tools

A default installation of the TCP/IP protocol suite comes with a protocol called Simple Network Management Protocol (SNMP). (Although it's installed by default, it's typically also turned off by default, especially with the Windows 95 family of operating systems.) We have already seen how much it can cost to perform a physical inventory manually, so let's investigate how much a few automated tools would cost in comparison.

First we should establish which of the two major types of inventory tools we'll be using. In general, tools are priced either on a cost/resource structure or an overall cost. If the software you've chosen is a cost/resource type, you'll need to balance the number of resources to be inventoried against the cost of the inventory tool and the information that can be gathered from it. Obviously an automated tool that costs more than the labor it takes to perform the same action is not a good investment. On the other hand, a tool that is actually cheaper than the amount of labor required to obtain the same results is a good investment. But here's an advantage of automated software inventory tools: They do not have the same error levels as human technicians. This may tip the balance in favor of automated tools.

One such tool (although definitely not the only one) is Belarc's Advisor software. It can be downloaded from Belarc's Web site at www.belarc.com. Once the software is downloaded and installed (the whole package can easily fit on a standard HD floppy disk), the inventory detection takes only moments to determine any number of components, both hardware and software. Using a standard component in the TCP/IP protocol suite, Belarc Advisor (along with most other inventory software) uses SNMP. Without a lengthy discussion, SNMP is the protocol channel that is used to exchange information between the Management Information Base (MIB) and SNMP-based software tools. The MIB is a standard component database loaded inside most network layer–conscious devices for determining and reporting the overall health of the devices.

Tips, Tricks, and Shortcuts

There are a number of ways to reduce the work that needs to be done for a network inventory. The easiest way is to always buy name-brand components, making this an organizational standard. Then all the equipment will have identical components and should perform similarly. The majority of the time needed to fix a problem is the diagnosis phase. If nonstandard components are used, the diagnosis phase is repeated with every network failure. If standard equipment is used, the time used for diagnosis on one system can probably be bypassed the next time. You could even be seen as being extremely efficient, especially if you act proactively before a number of identical problems arise. Standards also let you "lean on" the historical documents from the manufacturer. At least the manufacturer will know the specifications of its own components, given a lack of customization. Also, some manufacturers have downloadable hardware or software diagnostics that will determine the capacities of their equipment. Gateway, for example, has an online tool that can be used to look up the specifications of your computer if the serial number is known. It also has a software tool that can be downloaded to determine if there have been any changes after purchase— rather like Belarc's Advisor.

Some tools that can help with the inventory work are provided by the OS manufacturer when the default OS is installed. Because most computer users (90% or more) have Microsoft operating systems, let's use Windows XP Professional as our example. One tool provided by Microsoft is called the Device Manager. It can be activated by opening the System Control Panel or by right-clicking on the My Computer icon and clicking on Properties (see Figure 4.1). In fact, Microsoft has provided this tool in all operating systems since Windows 95. All of the hardware devices that have been either recognized by the system (Plug-n-Play) or have been manually installed by the

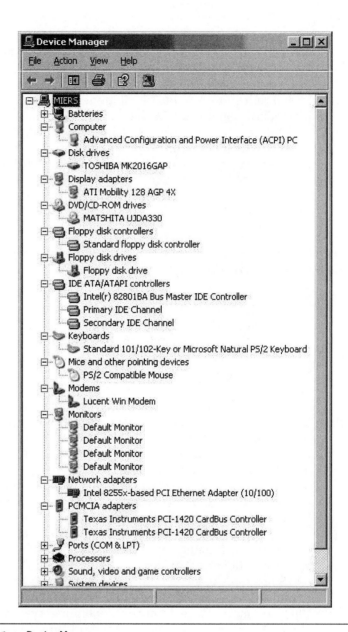

FIGURE 4.1 ◆ Device Manager

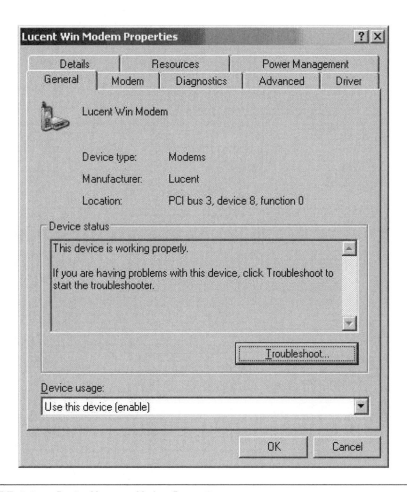

FIGURE 4.2 ◆ Device Manager: Modem Properties

administrator can be accessed through the Device Manager. Double-clicking on a specific device, such as the Lucent Win Modem installed on my laptop, allows the administrator to investigate the drivers loaded, the IRQ or I/O settings, whether the OS thinks the device is working properly, and so forth (see Figure 4.2).

One creative way to use the Device Manager is to print the specific information at installation. The printout is rather lengthy, typically 12 pages or so. But by having this information from the time of installation, the administrator has a historical document as a comparison if the manufacturer doesn't provide one. When I operated a small computer store, I used the Device

FIGURE 4.3 ◆ Printing the Device Manager

Manager (DM) printout (see Figure 4.3) as a hedge against users who can't help but customize their systems after they take them home. I always provided a warranty on our equipment and also provided free installation on equipment that we didn't sell as a customer service. But I had a DM printout as an insurance policy whenever there was some sort of billing dispute. This also works in the field if there is a device identification problem. Many manufacturers purchase components from other manufacturers, change the screen-printed logos, and repackage them under their own brand. This can make updating the drives difficult because of not knowing which set of drivers to use.

Another Microsoft-supplied tool is called System Information (see Figure 4.4). A more advanced and information-dense tool than Device Manager, System Information is where software goes whenever it wants to begin the installation process. SI is typically not that useful to the administrator, but the added functionality of the System History allows her or him to look back in time, seeing what has been installed, deleted, or modified since the installation of the OS (see Figure 4.5).

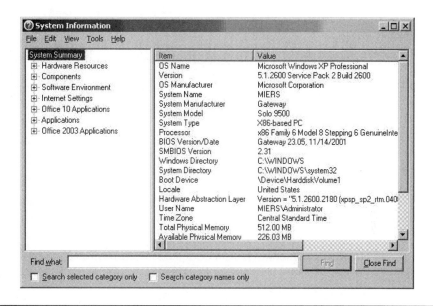

FIGURE 4.4 ◆ System Information

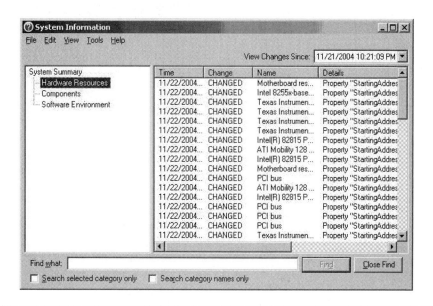

FIGURE 4.5 ◆ System Information: Changes

Summary

Although asset management may not be the most favorite or exciting task of a network technician or administrator, it is an absolute necessity. Without knowing what is part of the network already, there's no way to determine how this network should be performing or should grow. It's also likely that there will be some discrepancies, which will have to be accounted for.

Inventories can be both automated and physical/manual inventories. The automated inventories are obviously quicker, but they may miss vital components that either are not connected to the network or cannot be inventoried. Automated inventory tools may be more expensive, but they can put data into electronic format. Physical inventories are much more labor-intensive but often yield more accurate and concrete data.

Discussion Questions

1. Before continuing, guess the cost of the total network at your place of employment or school. (Don't be conservative; the total cost may surprise you.)

2. Perform a physical inventory of your department or school network. You may need to obtain the permission of the IT manager before performing this inventory. (*Hint:* One may have already been completed that can be used with your professor's permission.)

3. Take the physical inventory and put the data into a spreadsheet program or database. From this, research the approximate replacement cost for the devices and software listed. How close was your estimate in Question 1?

Business and Technology Analysis

5

Learning Objectives

After reading this chapter, you will be able to

◆ Define a business goal with the assistance of nontechnical staff.

◆ Relate a business goal to a network strategy.

◆ Complete a professional report of the analysis.

Why Is This Material Important to Me?

This chapter introduces one of the most powerful network design processes. Its power comes from its ability to condense the number of products under consideration from a vast ocean into the few that can work for the organization. This design process also provides a logical framework for obtaining management information about the company and the network's role in its continued survival and success. In short, business management strategy analysis allows analysts to design a network to better suit the needs of a company—instead of technology mandating how a business will adapt to it!

Introduction

Since humankind has faced decisions between options such as a wooden spear or a shaped stone to use in hunting, we have had to make a cost–benefit analysis. For instance, the wooden spear may be a better option, but it takes many hours to choose, shape, and practice with the wooden spear. The stone is a simpler tool, requiring much less shaping and time, but may not be as accurate as the spear. Of course, the weight of each of the advantages against the disadvantages can change based on your level of hunger. If your hunger is relatively satisfied, you will be more apt to go for the wooden spear. If you are exceedingly hungry, you will probably pick up whatever is handiest to satisfy that hunger.

Businesses also perform that type of analysis of their needs and resources. Most people are familiar with the term *cost–benefit analysis,* an accounting term that has merged into mainstream language. We will adapt the same philosophy to the networking and computer environment. Because techies typically don't understand the value of their expertise, most don't master the ability to communicate the strategic value of the technology at their disposal.

The format of the business and technology analysis (BTA) is not as important as the information it contains. As long as a thorough analysis has been performed and there's a clear, consistent style that is easy to read, almost any format is acceptable. Our format will be taken from James E. Goldman and Phillip T. Rawlings in *Local Area Networks: A Business-Oriented Approach* (ISBN 0471330477). Although this may be somewhat artificial in a real-world business, we're going to break our BTA analysis into five parts:

1. The business needs and budget available for the project.
2. The existing applications that must be maintained and supported by any new applications that need to be purchased and installed or configured.

3. The data format and traffic characteristics of the network.

4. The network architecture.

5. The technology available that can fulfill the first four analyses (this is a top-down analysis from management's perspective).

Some people find it easier to remember the BTA by its acronym BADNT. (No pun is intended referencing Microsoft's Windows NT.)

Management is ultimately going to decide whether to fund the project and its components, regardless of any merits that the "techies" recommend. The secret to secure funding for your network project, or at least to improve your chances to secure funding, is to perform a thorough analysis on a particular set of products or services showing the benefits of the project when weighed against the cost of implementation. If the project, product, or service will greatly benefit the organization, especially in the short term, it will be much easier to "sell." The BTA is one way for providing the framework for that type of analysis. For instance, we can filter a large number of vendors or manufacturers, let's say 250 or so, through the first four components of the BTA. By the time we process our final step, we should have only a handful of companies that can fulfill our needs. At the very least, we can compare the proverbial apples to apples. However, most techies do not think in this manner. Technical analysts tend to think from the bottom up, in a more functional manner, rather than from the top down. They see a technology, like it, are sold by its capabilities, and then try to find a business need for that technology. This is in stark contrast to the way that management thinks, which is in a more "big picture" way. We may be techies at heart, but we have to be comfortable operating in business and management guidelines to justify the purchase of our beloved technology.

To better illustrate the BTA process, let's go through a BTA with a sample business. Our example business is a small mortgage company, XYZ Home Mortgage, with seven employees. This analysis will seem fairly artificial, but it will illustrate the procedures that will be used throughout the rest of the text. Let's begin with what we know about XYZ Home Mortgage:

Known Facts

1. XYZ Home Mortgage has been in business for the past five years. The company was started by one mortgage broker/agent and has now grown to include six other mortgage brokers plus the founder, Bob Jones.

2. Because of the recent growth of the company, it needs a network. Currently XYZ lacks a server-based network and uses a Windows 98 peer-to-peer network.

3. XYZ is running a fairly standard Microsoft Office or other equivalent office productivity suites.

4. Bob Johnson has seen our ad in the local newspaper, talked with some of our references, and has approached us for a BTA of his current and future business plans and needs before deciding whether to hire our company or a competitor.

5. For any information that is not apparent, we will call Bob as our main contact.

In conversations with Bob, we have learned that he would like to have a network with a file server for file and print sharing. This will allow XYZ to have a central place for file access, maintenance, and backing up important files. He also stressed that the company is doing well now, but he expects a downturn in the economy, which means that funds will be fairly short.

Bob also stated that we shouldn't try to sell him workstations because those are in place. He's just looking for the server and the networking equipment. At this time we will need to include the workstations and the existing software in our internal BTA, but the final BTA should not assume they are established facts. We will be trying to get the installation contract, but we are hoping for a maintenance contract as well.

The Facts as We Know Them

Part One: Business Needs and Budget

XYZ Home Mortgage needs an upgrade to its existing network. Officially the existing workstations will not be part of the first bid; but if we perform a satisfactory analysis, we will probably be allowed to provide new workstations later. Bob has been guarded about the overall total budget for this project, but we will try to keep costs under $5,000, with the lowest overall costs being preferable.

Part Two: Existing or Needed Applications

XYZ is using Microsoft Office product suites and Peachtree accounting software, as well as Internet Explorer. We can try to convince the company to use different productivity suites such as Lotus SmartSuite, but if Bob and his company are familiar with Microsoft products it may be difficult to convince them to change. Customers' logic is rarely the same as technicians'. It's easy to lose customers because you appear to not understand their needs. This logic will also work with XYZ's accounting system, Peachtree. We may have a sense that XYZ is open to change, but their application software will not be changed in this initial network project.

It is often best in the applications part of the BTA to take one of two approaches. The first is to be as generic as possible by saying that XYZ needs a business productivity suite. The second is to be generic but list several industry-leading examples. "XYZ Home Mortgage will be using an office productivity suite such as Microsoft Office, Lotus SmartSuite, Open Office, or equivalent product."

Part Three: Data Formats or Network Traffic Characteristics

The files are currently shared across a peer-to-peer network between individual workstations. For instance, Bob has a list of potential customers within the files on his workstation. The other people can share his files through the existing network. These files are typical small—less than 2 MB. The transfer is relatively quick, so that's not going to be an issue once we have a network server installed. The other traffic on the network will be Internet traffic and e-mail.

Part Four: Network Architecture

Because this textbook is not focused on specific technologies, we will provide an overview but not explore the actual network architectures. Network architecture can be broken down into three components: access method (how the available bandwidth is accessed by the network devices, such as token passing or contention); logical topology (how the data gets from one end of the network to another on a conceptual level: broadcast or sequential); and physical topology (bus, ring, star, or mesh). It is important for our network engineers to know these components, but customers are typically not interested in the actual technology. Rather, they want to see the advantages a specific technology can offer. In most cases it would be inappropriate to include the following sentence in a customer BTA:

> After some deliberation, it has been decided that IEEE 802.3u is the network architecture that is recommended for this network. It has been chosen because of the contention-based [access method] packet broadcasting [logical topology] star-shaped network standard.

A much better statement might read something like this:

> After a careful analysis of the existing network architecture and future business needs, Fast Ethernet, otherwise known as IEEE 802.3u, is recommended. Fast Ethernet is readily available, possesses a relatively large bandwidth capability (100 Mbps), and is relatively inexpensive (compared to other comparable networking standards). While Fast Ethernet meets the current network requirements, it is also scalable to meet the needs of expected future growth.

It's a good business practice to tell customers what they need to know without overloading them with facts they don't really want to know. If they want to know more, they will ask, and it's your ethical responsibility to give them those answers to the best of your ability.

Part Five: Technologies Available

This section can start by stating our recommendations for the network, including specifications of available technology and product names. For this example, we might recommend Microsoft Windows 2003 Server because of its file and print sharing capabilities and because of the Microsoft Windows client workstations that are currently in the office. In contrast, we may feel that Novell Netware 6.x is a better solution for XYZ, but we know that Novell would not even be considered by Bob because he has repeatedly mentioned Microsoft Windows.

Unlike the applications section, in this section we should recommend specific applications such as Microsoft Office 2003 Developer Edition, describing the type of product instead of the actual product number. As an example, we might say that the client should purchase and install a workgroup-class router. What we do not want to say, even though it's tempting to do so, is to identify the *exact* product such as a Cisco 2511 router. Giving this piece of information away allows the client to purchase the product separately or even take your BTA to another organization to get a cheaper bid using your intellectual property. Actual product specifications and pricing will have to wait until the BTA has been approved; an actual bid would be the next step.

At this point we have enough of a framework to begin writing the BTA report in a narrative format. (Remember, information can always be added to the analysis as it is written.) It is also suggested, although not necessary, to have separate parts to the report for each part of the BTA. Use text formatting that makes it easy to distinguish between the different analyses. This allows readers to easily find their place in your analysis, especially if they are interested in a specific section.

This sample BTA has been artificially easy, with most of the facts and figures provided. In the likely event that needed information is missing, what can you do? This situation is not necessarily a matter of the company trying to keep information from you or your organization. The client may not know the answers, or you may not have asked the appropriate questions.

Although this hasn't been carved in stone, there are generally three approaches that work:

1. The best way to get information is to directly ask the customer liaison specific questions so you will have specific answers. Don't ask open-ended questions because you'll get nonspecific answers.

2. The next way is to perform a BTA with the available facts and then list any specific issues or concerns that were not adequately covered and need to be addressed for a more thorough analysis.

3. Alternatively, list the specific assumptions and then perform an analysis. Invariably such an analysis will be off the mark because of ambiguity, but it may be enough to convince a company that you understand the situation.

Example BTA for XYZ Mortgage
Business Needs and Budget

XYZ Home Mortgage was started five years ago with a single founder, Bob Johnson. Since then XYZ has grown to an organization of seven agents/brokers. While the needs of the organization are met by the current peer-to-peer network, the company needs a server-based network. Because the workstations and some of the users' software are currently installed and will not be part of the bid process, they will not be considered in this proposal. Although the budget is still to be determined (TBD), we will try to minimize costs.

Existing and New Applications

Although most of the workstation applications have been chosen and installed, it is recommended that XYZ should use a standard office productivity suite for word processing, spreadsheets, e-mail, and scheduling. Additional software includes accounting software and possibly industry-specific mortgage software. Without further clarification, no further recommendations can be made at this time.

Data Format / Traffic Characteristics

The majority of the data sent through the network will be Internet-related traffic such as Web browsing, e-mail, or some sort of instant messaging. The other traffic will be generated internally by file and print sharing. In short, the traffic characteristics will be generally small, bursty transactions rather than large, more sustained transactions.

Network Architecture

XYZ Mortgage is looking for a reliable, robust, easily expandable, and fairly inexpensive network. Because of market availability, available bandwidth, and ease of maintenance, the Fast Ethernet (IEEE 802.3u) standard has been chosen for this organization. Certainly other network standards would fulfill the needs of XYZ, but the availability and cost of Fast Ethernet make it the best choice for this company's unique needs.

Additionally, we recommend the use of a LAN switch or switches to facilitate the exchange of network packets between nodes. Historically, this could be accomplished by network hubs, but switches are a more cost-effective solution.

Technology Available

Several categories of specific technologies will be described in detail for each specific network function. The recommendations listed here are as accurate as possible given the information provided. Additional clarification would help to more accurately reflect the unique needs of XYZ Home Mortgage.

Network Server

XYZ Home Mortgage currently has a peer-to-peer network. As an upgrade, we recommend installing a file and print server for additional network performance and reliability. We recommend that a commercially available server, such as a SOHO-class server from a vendor such as HP, Dell, Compaq, or IBM, be purchased. Regardless of the choice of network operating system (NOS), the server should have a minimum of redundant hard disk drives, magnetic or optical backup device, and a minimum 1 GB of RAM. The requirements will be further analyzed once the network operating system has been chosen.

Network Operating System

The network operating systems currently available are of three major types. Although Novell Netware has been a reliable and robust NOS, and Linux has been shown to be a reliable platform, we recommend that XYZ choose the current version of Microsoft Windows or Small Business Server. The ease of use, user-friendly graphical user interface (GUI), and the overall market share make this recommendation the most appropriate for this situation.

Workstations and Operating Systems

The workstations should be of either home-class or SOHO-class specifications loaded with Windows XP Professional, not XP Home. (XP Home cannot be authenticated by a Windows NOS.) The amount of computing that will be performed on the individual workstations will not be of an extraordinary amount to warrant high-performance equipment. The existing workstations should fulfill these requirements adequately.

Workstation Software

The existing workstations are already equipped with the latest version of Microsoft Office. Although there are alternatives to MS Office such as Sun Microsystem's StarOffice (commercially available) or the equivalent Open Office (available for free download), XYZ is sufficiently comfortable with MS Office. As such, it is not recommended that any change is necessary.

It can be assumed that XYZ has an existing accounting system, such as Intuit's QuickBooks, PeachTree, or MYOB. Without further clarification, we will not be able to recommend specific accounting software.

It can also be assumed that there may be additional proprietary or industry-standard software for processing home mortgages. This may be either custom-published software, commercially available software, or a Web application (requiring only a standard Web browser).

Networking Devices

The access unit for the Internet, regardless of the monthly access type (see the Internet Access section), will be provided as part of the monthly service agreement. This unit will be connected to a commercially available residential broadband router (priced under $100). These broadband routers can be purchased in a variety of configurations, including built-in switching and wireless access. Additional network ports can be added through the purchase of additional commercially available switches (priced under $75).

Network Media

Fast Ethernet or IEEE 802.3u networks are typically installed using Cat5e cabling. The cost for the actual media is quite low (under $0.10/ft). Cat5e cabling, regardless of the manufacturer, provides more than enough bandwidth (up to 450 Mbps) for the Fast Ethernet standard (100 Mbps).

Internet Access

Although XYZ will not be providing on-demand access to its network externally, it is our recommendation that the company sign up for broadband Internet access with the local vendor of choice. The most likely choices for this service are either DSL (provided by the local telephone company) or cable (provided by the local cable TV company). Both services provide reliable Internet connectivity and satisfactory quality of service (QoS) and are fairly inexpensive (under $50/month). Both types of Internet service provide equivalent interconnection devices that provide network access between their network and XYZ's network. We would recommend broadband cable service, if available, because the available bandwidth is much greater for approximately the same monthly charge.

Purpose of the BTA Exercise

Until now the purpose of the BTA has been solely to influence the customer's decision to retain our firm to engineer and install computer or network equipment. Now we need to add a few other purposes to justify our efforts in this type of analysis. Not only is the BTA useful for the customer; it also helps us decide how we will actually install and engineer the network. Many times the BTA is actually an internal document used to narrow the scope of a project to more manageable size without being given to the customer. Rather, it becomes a part of the overall project documentation that will be kept in the organization's overall knowledge base.

Also, BTAs can be used internally between different departments or offices of the same organization. The process would be the same for internal customers as for external customers. It's not uncommon to have a set of BTAs ready for possible future company projects, which can be taken off the shelf, dusted off, modified, and presented without having to recreate the entire BTA from scratch. Many companies also have predefined templates, which also help begin the BTA process. This has been seen in an entirely different context over the past decade or so. The U.S. military has prepared many diverse military plans ranging in scope from securing a small village in an Eastern European country to overthrowing the government of a Middle Eastern country such as Afghanistan or Iraq. These contain the same types of analyses as our BTAs with several components that our civilian analyses do not, such as technical feasibility and overall political desirability of both the military action and the resulting outcome. Whenever a situation comes along that is sufficiently similar to a plan, which has already been planned, the preexisting plan is taken off of the shelf, dusted off, and modified to more closely match the current situation. A BTA is also a method for measuring the analytical skills of a new employee or management candidate looking for a promotion. It's not unheard of to present a "mock" scenario to use in the selection/promotion process for either potential employees or employees seeking promotion.

Note: The following example shows how I present and define the requirements for BTAs to my students. You can see how the specific requirements for an educational exercise are not the same as those of an actual corporation, but the overall product is similar.

Introduction

Due to the nature of the industry, a lecture and laboratory course would not expose the student to the wide range of technology, implementation, administration, and the like that exist outside the classroom. A major component to the DeVry Network and Communication Management degree is the management portion. This BTA is an attempt to include more network design and technical writing and better prepare students for the real-world environment.

Purpose

The purpose of these reports is to reinforce the importance and general mechanism of approaching an organization's business needs in a systematic and defensible manner. Within this framework, the analysis will be performed using the top-down business model, also known by its acronym BADNT. Consider each of these smaller assignments as chapters or sections of the final report to be presented as a whole later.

Deliverables

Each group should pick just one of the companies or organizations for which to perform the analysis and subsequent reports. Each research report should be typed and turned in every Friday afternoon at the close of business. These should be professional-looking reports suitable for compilation into a major report for the course. When all individual research reports are completed, they will be compiled into a single report covering the following areas: business needs and budget; applications—existing or needed; data format and traffic characteristics; network architecture; and technology available.

The group will be graded on report content, technical writing style, presentation style, oral presentation, and so forth.

Summary

Unlike some of the other preliminary topics, the business and technology analysis (or cost–benefit analysis) has a practical, if somewhat unseen, application within network design. It forces the design team to consult with client management and develop a communications channel and relationship with nontechnical staff. Analyzing the network from a business perspective generates results that are closely aligned with the needs of the organization that will be using and paying for the network.

Discussion Questions

1. After conducting a physical inventory, you have been given a mandate to develop a technology plan for the next five years. What information would you need to get started? Whom would you ask for this information?

2. Your boss is already frustrated about the amount of time and energy used on an inventory of the company's digital assets. Now you're coming to her with this whole BTA issue. How would you convince her to let you perform this analysis?

6

Computer Professionals Unlimited, Inc.

Learning Objectives

After reading this chapter, you will have

- An introduction to the model organization to use throughout the rest of this text.

- A brief overview of the model organization and its employees.

Why Is This Material Important to Me?

CPU, Inc., is a fictional company we'll be using as our model. From this point, the text will be written in a more interactive, time-based manner. For instance, there will be scheduled meetings, deadlines, and projects. Clients will be introduced and personalities explored. It is the author's intent to make these next chapters as alive and real-world as possible.

One thing that should become apparent from this type of exploration is the amount of network design that is out of the hands of the network designers. For example, the best network component for Network A might be Router Z, but the organization's IT department has a contract with the company that manufactures Router Y. Because of this contract (which includes special pricing and service), the branch office must install Router Y and design its network around its capabilities and limitations.

The Process

This text is not intended to be a complete book of network design, but it will introduce one of many possible methodologies or processes to accomplish client interactions and network design. It is also not intended to be a management or customer–management type of text. Simply put, the goal of this text is to provide a framework that allows for effective network design without being a network engineer.

To begin, we will establish the appropriate backstory to give these exercises a more authentic feeling. We, the readers and author, are going to play the part of John Dougan, network engineer for Computer Professionals Unlimited, Inc., otherwise known as CPU. CPU was started as an extension of an undergraduate senior project. During this exercise the team was required to find an external client who needed some network-related work completed for his or her organization. While adequate, the coursework at the university did not really prepare the team for the complex and often uncharted corporate world. After their project was completed, they decided to apply what they had learned, and formed CPU. The organizational chart (see Figure 6.1) shows how the company has been set up.

During a networking class the future CPU employees were taught a business process that they found interesting: the top-down business model or BTA report (further described in Chapter 5), put forth by James E. Goldman and Phillip T. Rawlings in *Local Area Networks: A Business-Oriented Approach* (ISBN 0471330477). The process resonated with them—specifically the aspect of modeling the network around the business needs of the organization or client. Unlike how most self-described techies work, this model begins with business needs. After they are thoroughly analyzed, the technology that can

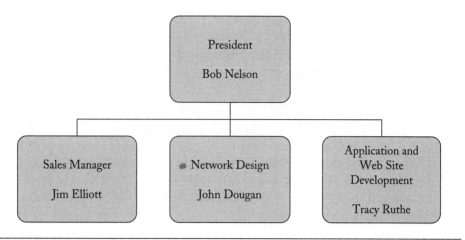

FIGURE 6.1 ♦ CPU Organizational Chart

best serve those needs is researched. This top-down business model is a management-oriented analysis. It is designed in such a way that the management team, which usually doesn't have the same depth of knowledge about computers as the IT staff, is involved in the network design process and has a better understanding of the resulting network.

Always remember that it's the management team who must be persuaded to release the funding that allows us to do our jobs and buy the technology that we love to play with!

Assimilating the BTA into CPU's company policies, Jim Elliott further expanded the academic model into a more practical customer relations process. After the initial contact (a telephone call, e-mail, personal meeting, or the like), Jim and his associates begin with the available facts and then start the building process for the BTA. Again, the BTA is not a magical process but more of a convenient and linear way of collecting thoughts for a more productive and error-free final product. After the first draft of the BTA has been written, any ambiguities or lack of facts become more apparent and should be addressed by direct communications with the client. The first draft BTA is then revised to include the new information. This process continues until the design team, headed by John Dougan, is confident enough to implement any of the BTA's conclusions.

Routinely, CPU also begins the design phase alongside the BTA process. These activities actually help to facilitate each other. If there is a glaring design issue, the appropriate fix or workaround can be put into the BTA and vice versa. A project bid is also worked on by Jim to facilitate the BTA and network design activities. Here's the catch: Only the BTA will be turned in until the client hires CPU to perform the actual project. The rest of these documents are for internal use only. The client will receive a client-only set of documents either during the design phase or after the project has been completed. It's not the way everyone does things, but it's worked well for CPU. This approach also removes the overriding desire for only the lowest possible bid being considered. Our company has prided itself on providing the finest quality network service while also remaining reasonably priced. Allowing the bid to be released only after the BTA is approved allows creativity and innovation to be at center stage instead of just the initial cost.

An interesting case study against choosing the lowest bid can be seen surrounding the events of the rocket booster assembly built by Morton-Thiokol (http://onlineethics. org/moral/boisjoly/RB-intro.html#vid) for the *Challenger* space shuttle. Robert Boisjoly, one of the chief engineers for MT, has a chilling minute-by-minute video case study available for viewing or purchase. It's definitely a must to see with the management and employees who want to exchange their integrity for a substandard project or working environment!

Throughout the project, the CPU-only documents go into a "completed projects" repository. These are kept for a number of reasons. One is for future auditing. Another reason is to have a copy so if a similar situation arises in the future, CPU won't have to reinvent the wheel (Remember last chapter's discussion of this topic?). Also, one copy of the client-only documents will be included in the completed projects repository with another set being sent to the client for their records. (Just don't get these sets confused and give the CPU-only and the client-only documents to the wrong parties! Document watermarks, separate file names, and separate file locations are always a good idea once the company standard has been created and adopted.)

Additional considerations throughout this process are troubleshooting and maintenance. CPU has found that if a network is originally designed with these two features in the forefront of the design, it will be easier to troubleshoot whenever the inevitable future problems occur. It will also be easier to perform routine maintenance on such a network.

Throughout the BTA process, CPU typically meets at least three or four times with the client to clarify requirements, strengthen professional relationships, and make sure the finished product is in line with customer demands. CPU also has a series of documents that are used to standardize projects for internal purposes. For instance, there is a standard client meeting form that will be completed, reviewed, and placed into the official project repository. These forms are just for internal use and will not be given to the client. Any changes to the requirements also have a form associated with them, referencing the client meeting form, so there is complete documentation with a project timeline.

Once a project has been approved, the bid process officially begins. For some companies bidding is a risky process. Because CPU gives the customer the BTA first, the bid process is much less risky because CPU has already built positive rapport with the customer and has a much better sense of what the client actually wants. This relationship puts CPU in a much better position, if not an almost guaranteed winning position throughout the bid process. CPU and the customer are "on the same" page and have probably conquered most of the hard decisions. While some contracts are awarded because of the lowest bid, a majority are awarded because of a meaningful and advantageous relationship between the customer and the contractor. This is the process that CPU has invested a lot of time to assimilate into its business processes. In addition, CPU has actually used the BTA development time as bid time as well. By planning the eventual network and the components needed while developing the BTA, most of the work for the bid was done at the same time.

A brief outline of CPU's process is as follows:

1. Initial contact with customer.
2. Begin BTA/bid process.
3. Clarify customer's expectations (usually three or four meetings).
4. Submit BTA.
5. Obtain BTA approval.
6. Submit bid.
7. Contact vendors.
8. Order materials.
9. Perform project installation.
10. Have clients sign off.
11. Wrap up project.
12. Perform postmortem.

Summary

CPU, Inc., was started as an extension of a class project. The principals have put together an organization that prides itself on fostering customer relationships throughout the bid process, as well as service after the bid has been accepted. Instead of using the traditional sales-oriented business model,

CPU builds relationships. Clients pick CPU because of its customer service, attention to detail, understanding of clients' needs, and ability to partner with clients. CPU clients come back because of the same reasons. Remember that happy customers tell other potential customers about your company, but unhappy customers tell everybody!

Discussion Questions

1. There are several different types of organizational models possible: project, matrix, and hierarchical. Which of these is used by CPU? Why do you think this type was chosen? (Even though these topics were not mentioned in the text, a little research at the library, on the Internet, or asking your instructor should give clarity to this topic.)

2. If given the chance, how would you organize CPU? How would your organization be similar to CPU? How would it be different? Be specific in giving your reasons.

3. There are risks inherent in conducting business as CPU does, compared to an organization that uses a more traditional bid process. What are some of the disadvantages for CPU? What are some of the advantages?

4. Research whether any industries use the same type of methodology as CPU. Do you know of any companies that use the CPU method of working with customers?

PART II

Target Organizations

Cross Creek Construction

7

Learning Objectives

After reading this chapter, you will be able to

- Determine the business needs of Cross Creek Construction for information technology.

- Given the business needs of CCC, develop an appropriate network design.

Why Is This Case Important to Me?

Many of my students, both present and past, have a misperception that large networks in major companies are just waiting for their skills after college graduation. Although this is certainly true, the vast majority of networks that require the most work are those found in small companies like sole proprietorships and small office–home office (SOHO) networks consisting of fewer than 25 computers. Organizations with larger networks will almost surely have a dedicated IT staff already in place. Such networks typically have their own design staff and use outside contractors to perform specific tasks such as installing a Cisco router network, installing cabling during a renovation, or redesigning their Internet presence.

As an alternative and more real-world example, this case study has been crafted to help you better understand how a network can be used as a tool to help an organization and not the other way around. Often overlooked, small businesses can be a viable source of revenue-generating IT projects. Another benefit from working with the neglected small business owner is the tremendous amount of word-of-mouth advertising and referrals that come from providing professional and honest service.

The Basic Facts

Organization:	Cross Creek Construction
Building:	Two different buildings: small central office and inventory warehouse
End users:	10–15 simultaneous connections
Budget:	$1,725
Basic requirements:	The customer would like to link the central office and the inventory warehouse together so that both the accounting and construction staff can eliminate some manual paperwork and forms. The connection doesn't need great bandwidth but must be able to withstand some interference due to cellular phones, electrical motors, and the like.
Analysis:	Give CCC two different analyses: the "best-of-the-best" network equipment and the "this-will-work-but-we're-not-proud-of-it" network equipment. Be sure to provide appropriate mechanisms and equipment for disaster recovery, unforeseen growth, equipment failure, and so on.

Our Audience/Our Customer

Before we begin, we will first try to understand our customer. Ed Pontier of CCC is a former full-time, hands-on carpenter who was displeased by the way his former bosses managed the projects he worked on. He thought they made everything too hard, didn't satisfy the customers, and tried to maximize profit to the detriment of the work quality. Possessing a "can-do" attitude that worked in his favor in the U.S. Marine Corps, he decided to start Cross Creek Construction. Over the years CCC has established itself as a small company that can be counted on to provide quality craftsmanship, always completing projects on time and on budget, with most projects being ahead of schedule and under budget. Ed's work philosophy is the same as the USMC: He's always looking for a "few good workers" and has to rely on his tools that have military-grade reliability. Into this environment CPU is to design, sell, and maintain a new solution that would change how CCC performs its business, without failure.

Business Conditions

CCC is a small construction company consisting of two buildings (a central office and an inventory warehouse) that are physically located on the same tract of land in close proximity (the buildings are approximately 75 meters apart). The central office is everything that could be expected in a construction office. It has three permanent employees with offices along with the capabilities for up to five other employees in a large communal office—usually temporary workers or contractors who are added whenever large projects warrant the extra staff. Also, there is a conference room where the whole crew and customers can gather to look over blueprints, have meetings, and so on. The warehouse is essentially a barnlike structure made of corrugated sheet metal with one large door for shipping and receiving and two normal doors for entrance and exit. This structure also functions as a makeshift workshop for the manufacture and assembly of certain projects such as cabinets and construction jigs, and occasionally as an automobile service center as well. In addition, there are two offices for administrative purposes. All in all, there's nothing unique about this setup, so our project shouldn't be that difficult due to specialized requirements.

Although this is a generally routine project, a number of factors certainly present challenges:

1. Mr. Pontier is not a computer or network expert, nor does CCC have employees with those skills. The computers and network need to be functional and reliable at the expense of performance.

2. The computer resources should be built with the inevitable breakage of components as a priority consideration. This is because of the harsh conditions that exist in this environment such as dust, dirt, temperature extremes, and the like. Also, there is a sense that the network will not be maintained according to the proper schedule: Mr. Pontier has said that they don't "fix nothing until it's broken."

3. Some of the network infrastructure can be installed either partially or completely by the employees at CCC, especially the burying of any backbone cable between the two buildings and even running the interior cabling.

4. There will need to be quite a bit of user education to make the customers satisfied with their new system.

5. Both the office and the warehouse are electrically noisy environments; a number of devices produce a wide range of electromagnetic interference. These devices could include cell phones, improperly maintained machinery, the metal structure of the warehouse, and even the electrical plant of the office and warehouse.

Customer Meeting 1: October 3

A meeting was set up for the first Monday of October between the principals of CCC and CPU, Inc. As we arrive at CCC, we get our first glimpse of CCC's facilities (see Figure 7.1), which were just as described. CCC is located at the edge of an undeveloped plot of land in an industrial park. We are greeted by Ed Pontier and his administrative assistant and are shown into the conference room.

After pleasantries have been exchanged, we begin our meeting. We ask Mr. Pontier to explain his exact situation and what he hopes to accomplish in this network project. He explains that his construction business has been very successful to this point. In fact, he confesses that his business has grown even though they have not actually been using their computers much except for e-mail and Internet surfing. They've been working up their bids, project specifications, and other business processes by hand. They've even been drawing up their plans using pencil and paper! Further, he feels that the lack of computerization is beginning to hurt his business.

To address this inadequacy, Mr. Pontier wants specific issues addressed. After the business needs are met, he does not want a complicated computer system. His employees are good at what they do, which is construction, and are not computer people. He realizes time will be needed for learning the new system; but if the transition is too expensive or lengthy, CCC will not be able to upgrade. Mr. Pontier's sentiment can be summed up by one statement he made during the first meeting: "Folks, I realize you're good at what you do, but if your computer network makes us less good at what we do, we won't be able to come into the 'Digital Age.'" At the conclusion of the meeting the standard goodbyes are exchanged and another meeting is set for two weeks—October 18, when the preliminary BTA and project specifications will be revealed.

Detailed Discussion of BTA Recommendations

After the first customer meeting, John Dougan starts to work on the first draft of CCC's BTA (see Document 1 at the end of this chapter) along with the network diagram and project bid. The initial draft is just a beginning point for negotiations and clarifications. During the second meeting, CPU will present its findings and recommendations in a nonthreatening manner.

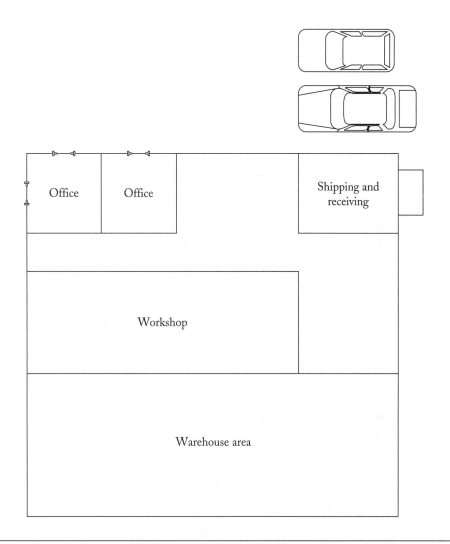

FIGURE 7.1 ◆ Land Plot (Visio)

Most of the recommendations are straightforward, especially the network standard (Fast Ethernet and Cat5e UTP cabling) and the network server running the current Microsoft Windows. Fast Ethernet with Cat5e cabling is the standard for residential, SOHO, and small network installations. The advantages of Fast Ethernet devices include their cost (as low as $25 for name-brand internal NICs and $30 for SOHO unmanaged switches), their high amount of bandwidth (up to 100 Mbps), and their availability (at common retail outlets).

TABLE 7.1 NOS Comparison

Characteristics	Windows	NetWare	Linux/UNIX
Ease of installation	Yes	No	No
Capabilities			
File sharing	Yes	Yes	Yes
Print sharing	Yes	Yes	Yes
User admin	Yes	Yes	Yes
Web server	Yes	Yes	Yes
e-mail server	Yes	Yes	Yes
Cost of installation	High	High	Low
Standard hardware	Yes	Yes	Yes
Interoperability	Yes	Yes	Yes
Native backups	Yes	Yes	Yes
Availability of support	High	Medium	Low

The arguments for Cat5e cabling include speed (up to 450 Mbps), ease of installation (terminated with standard hand tools), and relatively inexpensive purchase and installation (between $0.05 to $0.10 per foot). In fact, no competing type of cabling can exceed or even match Cat5e cabling.

The choice of Microsoft Windows is also fairly straightforward. Several server or network operating systems could be used for this network, including Microsoft Windows, Novell NetWare, and one of the various varieties of Linux. To make a more objective choice, CPU has taken several features into account, which are outlined in Table 7.1. To some, the deciding factor is the availability of local technical support. Linux may be free to download and implement, but technical support is expensive. This is especially true if you have to hire a specialist who is not local. At $100 or more per hour, eight hours of technical support eats the difference between the free download for Linux and the higher purchase price of Microsoft Windows.

The network server, being the component with the worst effect if something were to happen to it, should be a proprietary SOHO-class system with backup capabilities. This is not to say that nonproprietary systems such as "white boxes" or even "built boxes" are not worthy of being used. Because Ed Pontier said he wanted absolute reliability, proprietary systems will be chosen for this project. We will focus on systems built by such companies as Dell, IBM, Compaq, and HP, which have better service contracts, and even on-site repair.

If something goes wrong, these companies have standard models that help diagnose problems and local service technicians to quickly get a server back up and running.

Another consideration is the choice of storage devices. Many, if not most, servers have magnetic tape drives to provide long-term archival of precious data files. Although that strategy has historically been the best choice for medium to large networks, optical storage devices such as CDs or DVDs are ideal choices for small networks. Data that are archived will not be needed in the short term, but rather for a catastrophe or an audit much later. If the magnetic media cannot be accessed because the type of device is no longer available, the data will be of no value. Another disadvantage is the fragility of tape media. Think of the reliability of a floppy diskette and what circumstances can lead to data failure. These include but are not limited to temperature extremes such as freezing, or surviving a fire even in a commercially available fire safe; changes in humidity; proximity to magnetic fields; and so on. On the other hand, optical storage is not affected by environmental conditions except for temperatures high enough to warp the actual media and prolonged exposure to direct sunlight. Also, almost every system manufactured since the mid-1990s has a CD drive, with most now having the ability to recognize DVDs.

Customer Meeting 2: October 17

All participants arrive promptly at the prescribed time and place. After quick introductions, the meeting begins. Jim Elliott begins by restating the established facts from the first meeting and then launches into CPU's presentation (see the Student CD). About halfway through the "Applications: Existing and Needed" section, Ed asks Jim to stop while he confers with his office manager, Jan. Many business or network analyses stop at this point. Ed wants to make sure that Jan understands the implications of the applications recommended and whether CCC really needs such applications. After some consultation, Jan gives an approving nod. The recommendations of the "Data/Traffic Format" and "Network Architecture" sections proceed without much discussion. High-speed cable is not a possibility in this locality, but DSL is available.

The last point of discussion is the need for a server. To Ed this is an added expense without much benefit. It's difficult for him to understand the need for a piece of expensive equipment that no one will be using for "actual work." After we explain what a server's function is, why it's indispensable to CCC's overall goals, and what type of return on investment or ROI can be realized through the use of a server, he still doesn't like it, but he grudgingly accepts it.

At this point the main points of the BTA are basically agreed on, and it is agreed that CPU should "tighten up" a few issues, get some prices, and write an official project bid, which is due in two weeks. The appropriate changes will be made and resubmitted as a formality and as part of the permanent record.

Customer Meeting 3: October 31

Today is the big day. After the weeks of hard work, the team is going to be handing over the finalized BTA and the project bid for approval by Ed Pontier and CCC. Until now, CPU's been pretty secretive about how much this is going to cost and the actual details of the new network implementation. If CPU has done its job correctly by building rapport and establishing a good working relationship, the network bid should only be a matter of negotiation, not a hostile document.

The Student CD has a copy of the documents mentioned in the text. One of these documents is a Microsoft Excel spreadsheet to use in determining how much the actual network installation will cost along with the approximate markup on the different components of the network installation.

Network Installation: Basic Considerations

Since beginning the initial BTA, CPU has contacted its vendors and locked in both cost estimates and delivery times for the components that are not on hand at the office. Due to the success of past projects, CPU has good credit and cash reserves. This lets CPU obtain equipment and supplies on either a 30- or 60-day deferred billing or purchase outright while waiting for project bids to be officially accepted. On larger projects CPU could not possibly purchase all the components; but smaller ones could certainly be started by getting at least some of the components before the project is officially accepted. Not only is this a luxury, sometimes it's an absolute necessity. Vendors often run out of stock and are not able to replenish in time to complete a project. Many projects are compromised because of an inability to get parts, therefore making the projects late.

Another consideration comes from carpenters. They often say, "Measure twice, cut once." In other words, take the time in the beginning to make absolutely sure that a plan is well thought out and that everyone knows what needs to be done.

Network Installation: Actual Installation

CPU's technicians arrive on Monday, November 15, to start the installation. They have been given access to whatever resources are needed for the speediest and smoothest installation. Because a copy of the building plan (see Figure 7.2) was obtained during the BTA and network design phase, the technicians know almost exactly what they are getting into. They unload their equipment and parts into a small corner of the warehouse facility. This will be their mobile office for the next couple of weeks.

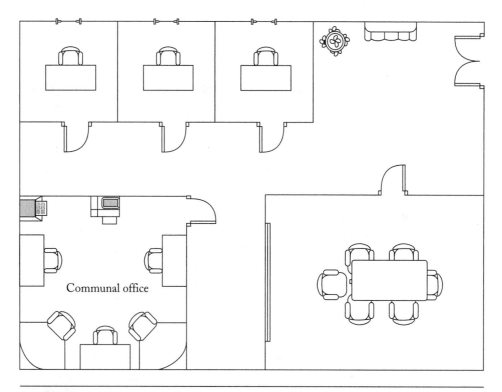

FIGURE 7.2 ◆ Building Blueprint

The wall ports, face plates, and drywall attachment brackets are distributed and taped onto the walls where they will be installed. The exact measurements for the lengths of cable are determined, along with plenty of slack for adjustment and ease of termination. The Cat5e is then pulled out of the box, cut to length, labeled, and laid on the floor approximating the layout after installation. These segments will be left for later installation by some of CCC's employees. The holes for the wall plate brackets are cut for easy cable installation. After the Cat5e has been installed, the ends will be terminated and the wall plates permanently mounted. If the termination is successful, testing with a network cable tester, such as a Fluke NetTool Pro, will confirm that the cabling is within IEEE standards.

The PCs are delivered from the vendor of choice on Wednesday. As an added benefit, these systems come preloaded with Windows XP Pro and Microsoft Office. After a final cost–benefit analysis, it was determined that this would be more cost efficient than getting a less expensive system and spending time installing the OS and the productivity suite. If the installation goes smoothly, installing and updating the OS alone could easily take two hours or more. That figure could easily double for installing and updating the productivity suite.

A name-branded or proprietary server is also recommended, as has already been discussed.

On Thursday, with the network cabling installed, the cabling is terminated and tested for network throughput. On Friday, the computer systems are distributed to the installation locations. The server is taken home for the weekend so the CPU crew can finish the server configuration and then "pop" the server down into the network and not have to spend that time next week, when everyone is waiting on the server. The systems are set up and connected to the network on Monday morning. By afternoon, they are being configured for the individual users. By the end of the day Tuesday each system has been tested for network connectivity and ability to access the network server. Training begins on Wednesday and extends through the close of business on Friday.

On the following Monday morning, the principals of both CCC and CPU meet to "walk through" the network. This allows CCC and CPU to discuss any lingering issues and to officially hand the final project documents to the customer. After CCC signs the client acceptance document, the employees from CPU leave for a long lunch. The client acceptance document is extremely important in both symbolism and legality. Symbolically, CPU can feel a sense of accomplishment and close out another project. Legally, CCC's signing the document means the project has been successfully completed to the satisfaction of CCC.

A final word of warning: Just because a project is officially completed, the work of satisfying the customer has not ended. Inevitably some unforeseen issue will arise. At these times CPU will serve the customer to maintain its professional reputation. It's much easier and cheaper to keep an existing customer satisfied than to gain a new customer!

Cross Creek Construction Timeline

Customer meeting 1	October 3
Customer meeting 2/initial BTA	October 17
Customer meeting 3/final BTA/project bid	October 31
Network installation	November 14
Project termination	November 28

Summary

- Cross Creek Construction is a successful but small construction company that is looking to expand its computing and networking capabilities.
- CCC wants a reliable and easy-to-maintain solution for its nontechnical employees.

◆ In business it's not always the best solution that wins the customer; rather, it's often the solution from the vendor who has the best relationship with the customer.

◆ Always look for easy and cost-effective ways to add unexpected value to exceed a customer's expectations.

Class Discussion

1. Using the information and formulas from the spreadsheet file on the Student CD, go to several vendors to obtain actual prices for the components used in this project.

   a. What is the lowest actual cost of the hardware needed to complete this project?

   b. What would be the cost of the hardware if CPU wants a 25% markup?

   c. What would be the lowest cost if the labor cost per hour were bid at $45/hour?

2. How would you change your bid for Ed Pontier if the highest amount CCC could possibly pay was less than your asking bid?

   a. By 10%?

   b. By 25%?

   c. By 50%?

3. How would you change the BTA and even the overall process if you were a part of CPU?

Documents

Document 1   Cross Creek Construction BTA: Initial Draft (Submitted October 2005)

———————————————— ◆ ◆ ◆ ————————————————

Business Needs
Cross Creek Construction is a successful construction company wanting to expand its computer and network resources to better facilitate its business processes. Currently there are no connections between the office and the warehouse. There are currently no computers or network systems within the organization.

Applications: Needed or Existing
Because there are no computers or network, there is currently no legacy software to support. A variety of work-related tasks, such as financial transactions, currently being done manually can be made easier or automated by software. Office automation can be accomplished by an office productivity suite such as Microsoft Office, Sun Microsystem's StarOffice or its open source equivalent OpenOffice, Corel WordPerfect Suite, or the like. Financial applications can be facilitated with such programs as Intuit's QuickBooks, Peachtree, MYOB, or Great Plains Software. Construction drawings and schematics can be accomplished by low-cost construction design software titles from Broderbund or professional products such as Microsoft Visio. Internet functions can be provided by Internet Explorer, Mozilla FireFox, or the Avant browser, which are all provided free of charge. E-mail communications can be accomplished by such free products as Outlook Express or the more costly Outlook.

Each of these product groups can be implemented separately, but most allow for integration after adoption. As the needs of CCC expand beyond its existing software, additional software can always be installed to add functionality.

Data/Traffic Characteristics
Although the actual network traffic of CCC's proposed network cannot be determined at this time, a close approximation is possible. Because of the relatively small amounts of network traffic sent through the network initially, such as e-mail, Internet browsing, and a few files to print, the overall traffic patterns will likely be "bursty" (not sustained over a significant time) and needing relatively little bandwidth. As network usage increases, the traffic will be "bursty" but still utilize relatively little bandwidth compared to what is available.

Network Architecture

Because of the relative simplicity of the network, industry-standard Fast Ethernet, also known as IEEE 802.3u, is preferred for this installation. Fast Ethernet was chosen for a variety of reasons:

1. Cabling characteristics:
   a. Local availability.
   b. Ease of installation.
   c. Low cost of bulk cable.
   d. Large bandwidth (100 Mbps transmission).
   e. De facto industry standard.
   f. Low total cost of ownership (TCO).
2. Devices:
   a. Local availability of network interface cards (NICs).
   b. Local availability of networking devices such as hub, switch, router, etc.
   c. Low cost of installation.
   d. Cross-vendor interoperability.
3. Reliability and fault tolerance:
   a. Individual connections to network devices assure fault tolerance.
   b. Long history of manufacturers producing Ethernet equipment.

Technologies Available

Starting at the bottom, CPU proposes the following components:

Internet Service

We recommend either DSL or high-speed digital cable, depending on whichever local service has the best reliability based on local customer interviews and published service level agreements (SLAs). An additional factor to aid in the decision-making process is to compare the amount of bandwidth/cost per month.

Network Cabling

We also recommend Cat5e twisted pair cabling for enhanced reliability in an electrically noisy environment and for the high amount of bandwidth possible. Cat5e is also relatively inexpensive to implement and install while providing adequate network bandwidth.

Connection to Internet Service and within CCC

Common residential or SOHO broadband routers such as products offered by Linksys or NetGear will allow a connection from whichever

Internet service is chosen, plus multiple connections for either wired or wireless connections.

Workstations

Standard business or SOHO-class workstations will be adequate for the needs of CCC now and in the near future. We recommend that a proprietary or name-brand server be purchased to add file sharing and printer sharing. Additionally, we recommend that Microsoft operating systems be installed on the workstations and the server for better interoperability.

Document 2   Cross Creek Construction BTA: Final Draft (Submitted October 2005; Changes Are in Bold Italics)

◆ ◆ ◆

Business Needs

Cross Creek Construction is a successful construction company wanting to expand its computer and network resources to better facilitate its business processes. Currently there are no connections between the office and the warehouse. There are currently no computers or network systems within the organization. *A major concern with implementing this network is the reliability and ease of use of this network.*

Applications: Needed or Existing

Because there are no computers or network, there is currently no legacy software to support. A variety of work-related tasks, such as financial transactions, currently being done manually can be made easier or automated by software. Office automation can be accomplished by an office productivity suite such as Microsoft Office, Sun Microsystem's StarOffice or its open source equivalent OpenOffice, Corel WordPerfect Suite, or the like. Financial applications can be facilitated with such programs as Intuit's QuickBooks *(which is being currently used by CCC),* Peachtree, MYOB, or Great Plains Software. Construction drawings and schematics can be accomplished by low-cost construction design software titles from Broderbund or professional products such as Microsoft Visio. Internet functions can be provided by Internet Explorer, Mozilla FireFox, or the Avant browser, which are all provided free of charge. E-mail communications can be accomplished by such free products as Outlook Express or the more costly Outlook.

Each of these product groups can be implemented separately, but most allow for integration after adoption. As the needs of CCC expand beyond its existing software, additional software can always be installed to add functionality.

Data/Traffic Characteristics

Although the actual network traffic of CCC's proposed network cannot be determined at this time, a close approximation is possible. Because of the relatively small amounts of network traffic sent through the network initially such as e-mail, Internet browsing, and a few files to print, the overall traffic patterns will likely be "bursty" (not sustained over a significant time) and needing relatively little bandwidth. As network usage increases, the traffic will *continue to* be "bursty" but still utilize relatively little *sustained* bandwidth compared to what is available.

Network Architecture

Because of the relative simplicity of the network, industry-standard Fast Ethernet, also known as IEEE 802.3u is preferred for this installation. Fast Ethernet was chosen for a variety of reasons:

1. Cabling characteristics:
   a. Local availability.
   b. Ease of installation.
   c. Low cost of bulk cable.
   d. *High* bandwidth (100 Mbps transmission).
   e. De facto industry standard.
   f. Low total cost of ownership or TCO.
2. Devices:
   a. Local availability of network interface cards (NICs).
   b. Local availability of networking devices such as hub, switch, router, etc.
   c. Low cost of installation.
   d. Cross-vendor interoperability.
3. Reliability and fault tolerance:
   a. Individual connections to network devices assure fault tolerance.
   b. Long history of manufacturers producing Ethernet equipment.

Technologies Available

Starting at the bottom, CPU proposes the following components:

Internet Service

We recommend either DSL or high-speed digital cable, depending on whichever local service has the best reliability based on local customer interviews and published service level agreement or SLAs. An additional factor to aid in the decision-making process is to compare the amount of bandwidth/cost per month. *DSL is provided by the local telephone company with between 128 and 512 kbps transfers, and high-speed cable provides between 1.5 and 3 Mbps; cable has the better bandwidth per monthly cost. Because of the lack of local availability of high-speed digital cable, we recommend DSL for this installation.*

Network Cabling

We also recommend Cat5e *or better* twisted pair cabling for enhanced reliability in an electrically noisy environment and for the high amount of bandwidth possible. Cat5e is also relatively inexpensive to implement and install while providing adequate network bandwidth.

Connection to Internet Service and within CCC

Common residential or SOHO broadband routers such as products offered by Linksys or NetGear will allow a connection from whichever Internet service is chosen plus multiple connections for either wired or wireless connections. *If wireless networking is chosen, security and electrical interference are major concerns.*

Workstations and Server

Standard business or SOHO-class workstations will be adequate for the needs of CCC now and in the near future. We recommend that a proprietary or name-brand server, *such as Dell, IBM, or Compaq,* be purchased to add file sharing and printer sharing. Additionally, we recommend that Microsoft operating systems, *such as Microsoft Windows XP Pro and Microsoft Small Business Server 2005,* be installed on the workstations and the server for better interoperability.

Document 3 Cross Creek Construction Project Bid (Excel Spreadsheet)

◆ ◆ ◆

Computer Professionals Unlimited, Inc.

Client	Cross Creek Construction
Contact	Ed Pontier
Project Number	051003-b
Document Number	4

Hardware	Product	Units	Actual Cost	Bid Cost	Profit
	Cat 5e cable (in feet)	750	37.5	93.75	56.25
	In-Wall Junction Box	7	52.5	131.25	78.75
	Wall Face Plates	7	17.5	43.75	26.25
	Wall Ports	14	49	122.5	73.5
	Patch Panel (wall)	1	250	625	375
	Broadband Router/Switch	1	75	187.5	112.5
Software			0	0	0
Labor	Network Installation	25	1125	2812.5	1687.5
	Server Setup	10	750	1875	1125
	User Training	20	1200	3000	1800
	Total Cost		3556.5	8891.25	5334.75

Computer Professionals Unlimited, Inc.

Client	Cross Creek Construction
Contact	Ed Pontier
Project Number	051003-b
Document Number	4

Category	Product	Units	Unit Price	Actual Cost
Hardware	Product	Units	Unit Price	Actual Cost
	Cat 5e cable (in feet)	750	0.05	37.5
	In-Wall Junction Box	7	7.5	52.5
	Wall Face Plates	7	2.5	17.5
	Wall Ports	14	3.5	49
	Patch Panel (wall)	1	250	250
	Broadband Router/Switc	1	75	75
Software				0
Labor	Network Installation	25	45	1125
	Server Setup	10	75	750
	User Training	20	60	1200
	Total Cost			3556.5

Red Bridge School District

Learning Objectives

◆ Determine the business needs of Red Bridge School District.

◆ Given the business needs of Red Bridge School District,
develop an appropriate network design.

Why Is This Case Important to Me?

First, you and your children may have been a part of a local public school system, and public tax dollars should be spent in the most cost-effective way possible. Second, unlike a traditional for-profit organization, public organizations do not have a profit margin or stockholders to hold them accountable because there is no sellable product. Third, the needs of an organization whose sole purpose is to educate, which means that the technology is a tool used to illustrate specific concepts and support the efforts of the educators, are very different from those of a for-profit or nonprofit organization. Finally, some schools receive grants that must be completely exhausted during the funding period or there will be a reduced amount, if any, during the next funding period.

The Basic Facts

Organization:	Red Valley School District (see Figures 8.1 and 8.2)
Building:	Three different buildings: Vo-Tech; administration; classrooms
End users:	500 simultaneous connections
Budget:	$35,000
Basic requirements:	The school district would like to provide instructor workstations and Internet access to each classroom. Student Internet access is to be provided in the library and three computer labs scattered throughout the buildings. The workstations have 10 Mbps NICs with RJ-45 ports. Assume that the workstations, servers, and associated systems are already in place and do not need to be purchased.
Analysis:	Give the school district two different analyses: the "best-of-the-best" network equipment and the "this-will-work-but-we're-not-proud-of-it" network equipment. Be sure to provide appropriate mechanisms and equipment for disaster recovery, unforeseen growth, equipment failure, and so on.

Our Audience/Our Customer

As with the Cross Creek Construction (CCC) project, we will first try to understand our customer. Red Bridge School District, regardless of the associated demographics, receives a large lump sum in the form of a grant. Grant monies are often renewable. Renewable grants are based on either need or performance. It is unlikely that the conditions that justified a "needs-based grants" will be corrected during the life of the grant. Many of these grants have additional and sometimes seemingly frivolous stipulations. The funds distributed with a grant may be reduced in the next period if they are not completely used during this period.

Unlike CCC, the school district doesn't have a single point of contact or approval. The approval process consists of gathering ideas from local school

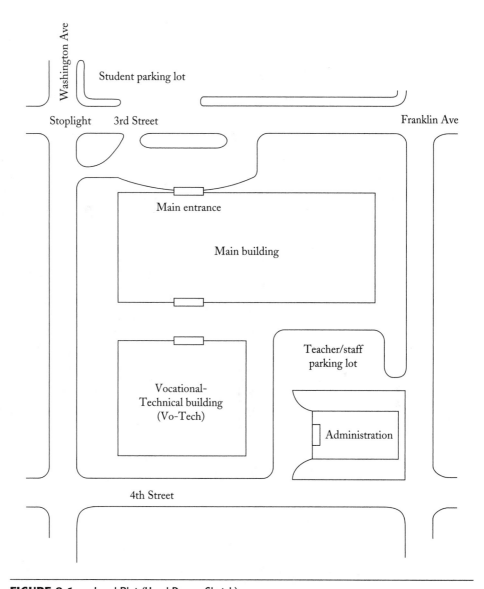

FIGURE 8.1 ◆ Land Plot (Hand Drawn Sketch)

personnel, submitting official requests to the administration, and getting approval from the school board. This can be either a lengthy and difficult process or a rubber-stamp process after gaining the approval of local school officials. Either way, the political conditions whenever you step into a taxpayer-funded institution can be tricky and downright hostile to change, so tread lightly!

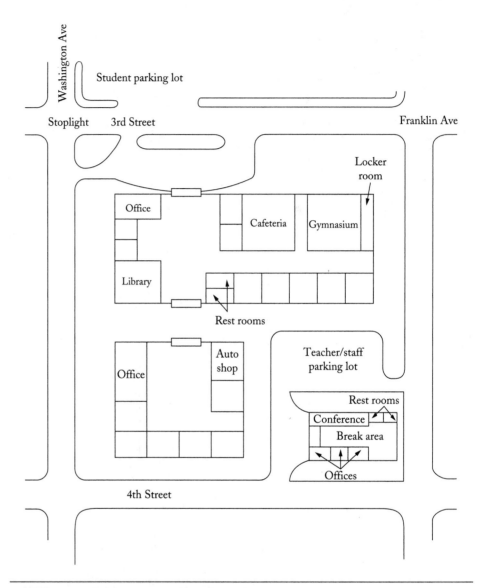

FIGURE 8.2 ◆ Building Blueprint (Hand Drawn Sketch)

Business Conditions

Red Bridge School District doesn't have the same type of business conditions as CCC. In fact, the school district doesn't have any "paying customers" per se. Because it is funded by the property owners of the local district, there is a different sort of accountability and customer focus. The school district really doesn't have a purchasable product, unlike a retail store or service provider. This fact changes the business focus. The computer network going down doesn't have such a major effect on the school district. There is also no way to quantify the cost of an outage because there is no visible lapse or degradation of service. There is also no method to determine how much having a better computer network would help the school district because there are no revenue statements to justify more expenditures.

Although the technical requirements are not terribly stringent because the school district is not a "production network," disruptions in network availability can complicate the educational work. As with CCC, there are a number of factors to consider:

1. Network segmentation will be a top priority. This will mean having many interconnected segments such as room or lab segments.

2. The more standardized the interconnecting devices are, the better. When an error occurs, it's much easier to troubleshoot a problem by being able to swap out identical components from one position to another.

3. No cost–benefit analysis can be performed for an educational facility such as the Red Bridge School District. The focus of for-profit businesses is to generate revenue that exceeds operating costs, making profit to justify the initial investment. Nonprofits do not have the same funding structure as a commercial company; taxpayers never see any financial returns on their tax dollars.

4. All funds must be used during the grant period. If the equipment can be used, the investment will actually be worth more than the dollar amount spent.

Customer Meeting 1: June 5

The CPU crew headed off to the first customer meeting with the Red Bridge School District (RBSD). Everyone met in the high school library. In attendance for the school district was technology coordinator John Leighton, high school principal Bob Dye, school library/media coordinator Linda Johnson, and a couple of the Vo-Tech computer teachers. After a few pleasantries, CPU asked what the expectations were of the network after installation. After a few moments the Vo-Tech teachers started to explain how much they could teach if they had a working network and how much of a benefit it would be to their students to have actually worked on a network. John Leighton, the technology coordinator, started speaking of his frustration in trying to keep all the computers in the district working and fixing problems in a timely manner. Linda Johnson expressed a desire to "pipe media into the classrooms." Although this was a good list of general guidelines, CPU needed more specifics.

The next question asked by CPU was "What would be the measure of success for this project?" After a few moments of deliberation, RBSD did not have any concrete or quantifiable desires except for the need for 500 or more simultaneous network or Internet connections. When asked more direct questions, the school personnel responded that they would be satisfied if the minimum number of connections could be maintained but also desired to show a benefit to the students such as extra training for the network technicians or an open house for both the students and their parents along with community leaders to see what improvements were made to the school facility.

Some generalities were traded back and forth and some "what-if" scenarios were contemplated. After a brief session of brainstorming, another appointment or meeting would be set for roughly two weeks from today. All agreed, and the meeting was adjourned.

Detailed Discussion of BTA Recommendations

John went to work on a first draft of RBSD's BTA along with the network diagram and project. As in the other cases, this was just a beginning point for negotiations and clarifications.

The Layer 1 or physical layer recommendations for the school district were basically the same as for CCC. The basic cable infrastructure would be Fast Ethernet and Cat5e UTP cabling inside the classrooms and throughout much of the overall network. The Layer 2 and 3 connection devices would be upgraded to switches. Between the buildings either Cat5e or fiber optic would be suitable, depending on the network traffic between the individual buildings.

Remember that network switches effectively do not share bandwidth and act as a single circuit between sending and receiving devices. Hubs, on the other hand, share their bandwidth between all systems that are connected to them. In essence, a four-port switch acts like four hubs of the same networking standard.

Unlike CCC, the school district would be using Novell Netware as its network operating system. This decision was made because of the comfort level that John Leighton, the technology coordinator, had as a certified Novell administrator (CNA). If John had to learn how to administer a Microsoft Windows server, it would add to his job duties and lower his productivity until he became as familiar with Windows as he already was with NetWare. Another factor was that NetWare, Linux, UNIX, and the new Mac OS X are more secure than Microsoft's Windows.

The security differences between the different operating systems come from their functional histories. Because a UNIX computer acts much like a centralized mainframe, users logged into it using a "dumb terminal." Because of that shared access with all files stored on the same physical unit, security had to be high. Novell NetWare continued the same type of security. Later Linux (an open-source variety of UNIX) also continued the same security philosophy.

For the exact opposite type of environment, Microsoft developed Windows NT for a workgroup environment. The applications for the individual users were primarily loaded on each local workstation. By design, the built-in security was lax because the only people sharing the server would be those working within the same working group or department. Since the release of Windows 2000 and its Active Directory Services (ADS), Microsoft has changed its overall security philosophy and built-in security.

The recommendation for the servers would also differ from that made for CCC. CCC needed only one server and could even function without an actual server if necessary. This was certainly not the case at RBSD. At a minimum, John Dougan, CPU's network designer, wanted one server for each building because of the amount of segmentation desired by the school personnel. These servers should be more robust than the one recommended for CCC. The minimum for these servers would be a business-class proprietary server (such as a Dell, IBM, Compaq, or equivalent) with 1 GB of RAM or so, redundant (duplicate and instantly available) hard disks, tape backup for data archiving (instead of the optical media drives recommended for CCC), and multiple processors or CPUs for better performance.

Besides the difference in the NOS, another major difference between this network and that of CCC is the amount of segmentation to be built in. To maximize fault tolerance, Dougan would like to be able to segment each classroom or laboratory into distinct subnets with individual room workgroup switches. This would allow a great deal of freedom for individual teachers to isolate themselves (sort of like closing their doors while lecturing) from the rest of the network if they would like to demonstrate network security without exposing the rest of the network infrastructure to any sort of hacking risk. This would also help in the functioning of the subnets if a catastrophe were to bring the server down. If each classroom had its own resources such as a printer and application access, the subnet could be self-contained until outside access was reestablished.

Similar to the CCC proposal, CPU would not actually install the network cabling. Instead a compromise was agreed upon. "What if some of the Vo-Tech and business students installed some of the Cat5e as a learning opportunity?" The concept was simple enough: Have a few CPU employees supervise or mentor the RBSD students. It would lessen the cost to the school district and help free vital CPU employees to work on other projects. This might help sell the project to the school board. Also, perhaps one of those students might want to work for CPU someday, or projects might be gained from this gesture of goodwill.

Customer Meeting 2: July 10

On the way through the school to the meeting room, John Dougan stole off to check on something, then reappeared with a twinkle in his eye. Unknown to the rest of the CPU group, there was an open trench that the electrical company had dug connecting all the buildings together. If that could be left open until after the campus backbone was installed, their job would be much easier! Dougan came in 15 minutes after the meeting started. (He had explored the trench to verify that it would work for the interbuilding networking cabling. The trench would be perfect for connecting the network across the three buildings.)

During the meeting the initial BTA was presented to the project stakeholders. The presentation went as planned with some quiet nods and fairly routine questions. The school staff were especially impressed by the degree of network segmentation within each building and across the entire network. The final surprise was how instrumental the students would be in actually performing the installation. Those students could gain many skills and some real experience. Although the network budget was not explicitly accepted, the BTA was accepted and thus, by extension, the network budget was also given the green light.

Customer Meeting 3: July 24

After weeks of hard work on both the BTA and the proposed training plan for the student workers, the finalized BTA and project bid were handed over to the administrators of RBSD. Here is a brief summary of the finalized BTA:

1. There would be a Layer 2 switch in every networked room.
   a. This would help contain network chatter between the devices in the room within the room's network. This is called *segmentation.*
   b. This would mitigate any network outage so that each network would be independent within the overall campus LAN. Although users might not be able to surf the Net, they could share files and printing while the rest of the network was down.
   c. Installing switches in every room would lessen traffic across the network infrastructure between rooms, between the rooms and the servers, and between the rooms and the Internet.

    d. Switches would also allow expansion within the rooms, provided they were purchased with a few open ports.

2. Between the buildings a fiber optic backbone would be installed connecting each of the buildings redundantly.

    a. Fiber optic was the medium of choice because of its high bandwidth capacity and resistance to both broadcasting and eavesdropping.

    b. Fiber optic was also preferred because of its ability to carry large amounts of data through a very small cable.

    c. Devices could be upgraded on either end without having to upgrade the fiber optic.

    d. Redundancy would sustain the integrity of the network when one or more segments were offline.

    e. During high network traffic, such as during a school competition or business tournament, the network traffic could be redirected through the redundant links.

3. Student workers would help install the cabling while being mentored by CPU network consultants.

    a. The Cat5e cabling would be installed within the ceiling, properly contained in cable management products. These segments would be installed, labeled, and tested for performance.

    b. The open trench currently on the premises would be used to install PVC pipe or conduit for the fiber optic between the buildings.

The Student CD has a copy of the documents mentioned in the text. One of these documents is a Microsoft Excel spreadsheet to use in determining how much the actual network installation will cost along with the approximate markup on the components of the network installation.

Network Installation: Basic Considerations

This network installation will be considerably different from that of CCC. There are a number of reasons for these differences:

1. There is no single point of contact or approval for this project. If changes need to be made, the amount of paperwork could be mountainous. This means that the project scope should be well defined, along with the actual requirements and the measures of success.

2. Part of the installation may be conducted by noncertified technicians.

3. All of the funds from the grant must be spent. If the funds are not used, they will be lost. On the other hand, if CPU overshoots the budget, there will be no other money available.

4. Once finished, this network will be considered a showpiece for the district and possibly other districts who desire to emulate this project.

5. The sheer size of this installation makes it somewhat of a monster for such a small organization as CPU.

Network Installation: Actual Installation

For two weeks or so before the installation, CPU has been mentoring and training the RBSD students who will help with the project. The RBSD students have been trained in cabling, testing, and labeling. Contingency plans have been formalized, documentation procedures have been developed, and communication guidelines have been developed and exercised. In short, the students have been more or less "CPU-certified" to work on the project to the standards of the rest of the CPU crew.

There are two schools of thought about industry certifications and standards. To some people certifications are an essential part of the educational process to display at least a minimum standard of proficiency for a set of skills. Others view certifications as artificial and somewhat misleading.

The author believes that certifications should be combined with experience. On the other hand, individuals with lots of experience but no certifications tend to be passed over for interviews and promotions even though they typically know the "by-the-book" methods.

Network Installation

CPU's technicians and RBSD students arrive on Monday, August 8, to begin the installation. During the past two weeks the project materials have been delivered to RBSD and staged on the locked high school cafeteria floor. This helps give an accurate inventory before beginning and also after project completion. The inventory is completed, the documentation paperwork is given out, and the formal project chart is drawn onto the whiteboard that has been temporarily installed for the project. These items help keep everyone on task and within the communications loop.

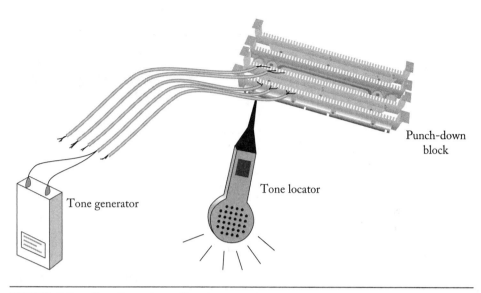

Punch-down block

Tone locator

Tone generator

FIGURE 8.3 ◆ Tone Generator and Locator

After lunch, the inventory is dispersed into location groups, where it will stay until being delivered to the individual rooms for installation. The cable runs are measured and remeasured for accuracy. The cables are cut to length (plus a little extra to compensate for unforeseen circumstances) and laid out on the floor where they will be eventually run through the ceilings to their destinations. So ends the first day of the installation.

Throughout the rest of the week, the cables are installed into the ceilings from the telecommunications closets to their destination classrooms. Each cable is identified using a tone generator and locator (see Figure 8.3).

Tone generators send an audible electrical tone through a cable on one end so the other end of the cable can be located among many other cables.

After identification, the cables are terminated with standard telco crimpers (see Figure 8.4) and tested with performance testers (see Figure 8.5). One end of each cable is terminated into a patch panel (see Figure 8.6), and the other end is terminated and inserted into a standard TIA/EIA outlet (see Figure 8.7). The resulting network looks like the typical UTP cabling installation (see Figure 8.8).

FIGURE 8.4 ◆ Standard Telco Crimpers

While the interior cabling is being installed, a team of students has been installing the PVC conduit in the open trenches between the buildings. After the conduit is installed, the cable is pulled through the conduit to connect the buildings together. In one of our bids the campus backbone is connected through fiber optic cabling, which allows much longer cable segments. In the other bid the backbone is connected using Cat5e UTP, which significantly limits the length of cabling to 100 meters or approximately 328 feet.

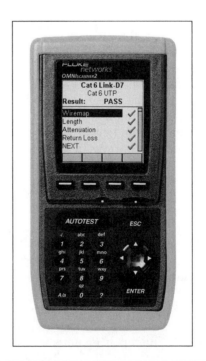

FIGURE 8.5 ◆ Performance Tester

FIGURE 8.6 ◆ Patch Panel

PVC conduit is the most cost-effective and desirable material for this type of under-ground (and even indoor) installation. The ease of connecting the PVC pipe is also a consideration for this type of installation. PVC pipe can be found in various lengths with diameters from ¼ inch to well over 6 inches. It is easy to couple PVC by first using a chemical cleaning agent and then using a chemical glue to adhere the pieces together. This makes a waterproof, practically crushproof conduit that is relatively easy to assemble.

While the network cabling and underground conduit are being installed, another crew installs the patch panels and switches in the wall-mounted equipment racks in each room. The exact locations of the equipment racks have been determined; the holes have been drilled and the racks affixed to the wall under the supervision of the maintenance staff.

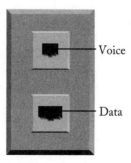

FIGURE 8.7 ◆ Standard TIA/EIA Outlet

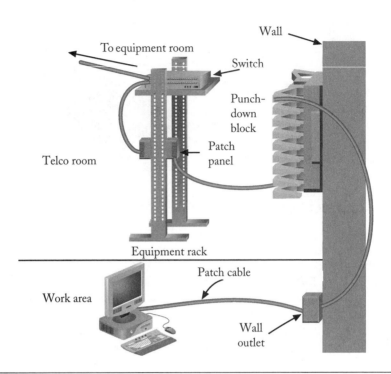

FIGURE 8.8 ◆ Typical UTP Cabling Installation

The building telco closets have been more problematic. The maintenance staff have had to carve out space from one existing classroom in each building to install the free-standing network racks. Unlike the smaller wall-mounted versions, these will be permanently bolted to the floor and walls and electrically grounded and will take up quite a bit of floor space.

The servers arrive on Tuesday of the first week of the installation. Because they were purchased with the server OS already installed, only the configuration needs to be completed before they are fully operational. Each user or group of users will have the following information: username; password; e-mail address; user's home directories; systems that can be logged into; login hours; applications restrictions; and so on.

The backup regimen must also be decided on, configured, and tested. This is the step where many organizations stumble. It's fairly easy to configure a backup device, but what should be backed up and where should it be stored? Only the actual data should be backed up. (Many organizations back up the OS and the applications, but these are easily replaceable.) The next step is to verify that the backups are viable or ready to use. Just as important is the storage of the backups. Many organizations store their backups onsite but in a different room or building. The proper place for data backups is offsite or at another physical address, preferably far enough away to protect the data from whatever disaster might strike at the organization's location. Another alternative is to store the data in a secure facility such as a storm shelter or bomb shelter.

After the Installation

The entire network is checked, rechecked, "certified," and completely documented. Invitations are sent to the project stakeholders, school administrators, and school board members for the project close-out and unveiling of the network to the public. The completed project documentation is formally turned over to the client and the client acceptance papers are signed, meaning that CPU has fulfilled its contractual obligations. The students are given credit for helping with the installation.

Red Bridge School District Timeline

Customer meeting 1	June 5
Customer meeting 2	July 10
Customer meeting 3	July 24
Network installation	August 7
Project completion	August 25

Summary

The business needs of the Red Bridge School District (RBSD) are substantially different from those of Cross Creek Construction. Instead of being a for-profit business, RBSD is a nonprofit organization that doesn't produce a marketable "product." This significantly changes how RBSD justifies its network design and its purchases. Also, RBSD has just received a grant to upgrade its network equipment. RBSD's network will need significant segmentation provided by individual workgroup switches in each room. Thus if the network has an issue, the individual rooms can be separated as their own room-sized LANs. RBSD is also different from CCC because there are three buildings with several hundred simultaneous network connections instead of two buildings with fewer than two dozen simultaneous connections. All these factors have contributed to a much different network design for RBSD than CCC.

Discussion Questions

1. Using the documents from Chapter 7 as a template, develop CPU's PowerPoint presentation. How would you change the presentation to the unique needs of RBSD?

2. Using the spreadsheet from Chapter 7 as a template, develop a network bid using the information contained within both BTAs to determine the overall cost of the project. Can the project be completed with the allotted budget? If not, what can be either deleted from the project or replaced with less costly products?

3. At the open house some school board members question your specific recommendations, such as fiber optic cabling between buildings and room segmentation for the network. It is evident that they don't approve of how the network was designed or installed. How would you justify your recommendations?

4. After purchasing all the network components you determine that there will be a substantial grant amount left over. What would be your recommendation for what to do with the excess if it was $2,000, $5,000, or $10,000?

5. RBSD has decided that it doesn't want to use Microsoft server products such as Windows Server 2003. What alternatives would you suggest, and why?

Documents

Document 1   RBSD BTA Final Draft—"Best of the Best" Version

♦ ♦ ♦

Business Needs

Since its establishment, Red Bridge School District (RBSD) has promoted the delivery of education through the most progressive methods. As such, RBSD has been on the leading edge of innovations and technological advances. In accord with this philosophy, the administrators have received a substantial grant from the U.S. Department of Education for the implementation of a network to interconnect the three buildings on the campus to further the education of students.

Applications: Needed or Existing

Several classrooms have individual computers, and a few laboratories have several (fewer than five) computers each. There is no existing network except between computers within the same room. The scope of this project will not be to install or even recommend the educational programs but rather to recommend network-related software such as server operating systems. The server operating system or NOS (network operating system) should have the following abilities:

1. File sharing.
2. Printer sharing.
3. E-mail serving.
4. Single logon capability for users who travel throughout the network.

Office automation can be accomplished by an office productivity suite such as Microsoft Office, Sun Microsystem's StarOffice or its open source equivalent OpenOffice, Corel WordPerfect Suite, or the like. Internet functions can be provided by Internet Explorer, Mozilla FireFox, or the Avant browser, which are all provided free of charge. E-mail communications can be accomplished by such free products as Outlook Express or the more costly Outlook.

Notice the similarities between this part of the applications portion of the BTA for RBSD and the one for CCC. If you have something that works, why not reuse it?

Data/Traffic Characteristics

The network traffic of RBSD will be rather bursty and will consist primarily of Web traffic such as Web browsing and e-mail, as well as files being transferred from the network servers and to printers. This traffic will not be sustained but will peak at the beginnings and at the end of the class periods. Because of the bursty nature of the overall network traffic, the required bandwidth of the network will be relatively small compared to what will be available, regardless of the eventual network cabling.

Network Architecture

Fast Ethernet or 100BaseT (IEEE 802.3u) was chosen for the connections to the workstations for a variety of reasons:

1. Cabling characteristics:
   a. Local availability.
   b. Ease of installation.
   c. Low cost of bulk cable.
   d. Large bandwidth (100 Mbps transmission).
   e. De facto industry standard.
   f. Low total cost of ownership or TCO.
2. Devices:
   a. Local availability of network interface cards (NICs).
   b. Local availability of networking devices such as hub, switch, router, etc.
   c. Low cost of installation.
   d. Cross-vendor interoperability.
3. Reliability and fault tolerance:
   a. Individual connections to network devices ensure fault tolerance.
   b. Long history of manufacturers producing Ethernet equipment.

Gigabit Ethernet or 1000BaseT (IEEE 802.3ab) will be used as both the intra-building and interbuilding backbone. This was chosen for many of the same reasons that Fast Ethernet was chosen for the individual workstation drops, with the added benefits of being highly resistant to electrical interference and having much higher bandwidth capacity.

The interbuilding LANs will be connected using Cat5e UTP for both simplicity and cost effectiveness. The individual wall drops will be run to a centralized patch panel and then to a 10/100/1000 Mbps workgroup switch. The individual room switches will be uplinked to the telco closets using a fiber optic cable. The individual buildings will be connected using redundant fiber optic links to ensure constant uptime.

Technologies Available

Starting at the bottom, CPU proposes the following components:

Internet Service

We recommend either DSL or high-speed cable, depending on whichever local service has the best reliability based on local customer interviews and service level agreements/SLAs. An additional factor is to compare the amount of bandwidth/cost per month.

Network Cabling

We also recommend Cat5e twisted pair cabling for enhanced reliability in an electrically noisy environment and for its high amount of possible bandwidth. Cat5e has also been shown to be relatively inexpensive to implement and install while providing adequate network bandwidth. We also recommend the use of fiber optic cabling as the backbone medium of choice for the segments between telco closets and the individual buildings.

Connection to Internet Service and within RBSD

For the number of network connections and the amount of Internet traffic, common residential broadband services will not be sufficient. The local service providers will need to be checked for the availability of business-class broadband services that will be accessed through enterprise-grade routers such as products offered by Cisco Systems, Nortel, or the like.

Networking Devices

Each individual room will be equipped with individual patch panels and 10/100 Mbps workgroup switches with 1000 Mbps fiber optic uplinks to the telco closets. The individual buildings will be equipped with redundant fiber optic cable runs to ensure maximum uptime connected through business-class routers such as those available from Cisco Systems, Nortel, or the like.

Workstations

Standard business or SOHO-class workstations will be adequate for the needs of RBSD now and in the near future. We recommend that a proprietary or name-brand server be purchased to add file sharing and printer sharing. Additionally, we recommend that Microsoft's current business-class operating system such as Windows XP Pro be installed on the workstations and the server for better interoperability.

Document 2   RBSD BTA Final Draft— "We're Not Proud of It" Version

—————————————————— ◆ ◆ ◆ ——————————————————

Business Needs

Since its establishment, Red Bridge School District (RBSD) has promoted the delivery of education through the most progressive methods. As such, RBSD has been on the leading edge of innovations and technological advances. In accord with this philosophy, the administrators have received a substantial grant from the U.S. Department of Education for the implementation of a network to interconnect the three buildings on the campus to further the education of students.

Applications: Needed or Existing

Several classrooms have individual computers, and a few laboratories have several (fewer than five) computers each. There is no existing network except between computers within the same room. The scope of this project will not be to install or even recommend the educational programs but rather to recommend network-related software such as server operating systems. The server operating system or NOS (network operating system) should have the following abilities:

1. File sharing.

2. Printer sharing.

3. E-mail serving.

4. Single logon capability for users who travel throughout the network.

Office automation can be accomplished by an office productivity suite such as Microsoft Office, Sun Microsystem's StarOffice or its open source equivalent OpenOffice, Corel WordPerfect Suite, or the like. Internet functions can be provided by Internet Explorer, Mozilla FireFox, or the Avant browser, which are all provided free of charge. E-mail communications can be accomplished by such free products as Outlook Express or the more costly Outlook.

Data/Traffic Characteristics

The network traffic of RBSD will be rather bursty and will consist primarily of Web traffic such as Web browsing and e-mail, as well as files being transferred from the network servers and to printers. This traffic will not be sustained but will peak at the beginnings and at the end of the class periods. Because of the bursty nature of the overall network traffic, the required bandwidth of the network will be relatively small compared to what will be available, regardless of the eventual network cabling.

Network Architecture

Fast Ethernet or 100BaseT (IEEE 802.3u) was chosen for the connections to the workstations for a variety of reasons:

1. Cabling characteristics:
   a. Local availability.
   b. Ease of installation.
   c. Low cost of bulk cable.
   d. Large bandwidth (100 Mbps transmission).
   e. De facto industry standard.
   f. Low total cost of ownership or TCO.
2. Devices:
   a. Local availability of network interface cards (NICs).
   b. Local availability of networking devices such as hub, switch, router, etc.
   c. Low cost of installation.
   d. Cross-vendor interoperability.
3. Reliability and fault tolerance:
   a. Individual connections to network devices ensure fault tolerance.
   b. Long history of manufacturers producing Ethernet equipment.

The interbuilding LANs will be connected using Cat5e UTP for both simplicity and cost effectiveness. The individual wall drops will be run to a centralized patch panel and then to a 10/100 Mbps workgroup switch. The individual room switches will be uplinked to the telco closets using Cat5e UTP. The individual buildings will be connected using single Cat5e links.

Technologies Available

Starting at the bottom, CPU proposes the following components:

Internet Service

We recommend either DSL or high-speed cable, depending on whichever local service has the best reliability based on local customer interviews. An additional factor is to compare the amount of bandwidth/cost per month.

Network Cabling

We also recommend Cat5e twisted pair cabling for enhanced reliability in an electrically noisy environment and for its high amount of possible bandwidth. Cat5e has also been shown to be relatively inexpensive to implement and install while providing adequate network bandwidth.

We also recommend the use of Cat5e UTP cabling as the backbone medium of choice for the segments between telco closets and the individual buildings.

Connection to Internet Service and within RBSD

For the number of network connections and the amount of Internet traffic, common residential broadband services will not be sufficient. The local service providers will need to be checked for the availability of business-class broadband services that will be accessed through enterprise-grade routers such as products offered by Cisco Systems, Nortel, or the like.

Networking Devices

Each individual room will be equipped with individual patch panels and 10/100 Mbps workgroup switches with 100 Mbps Cat5e uplinks to the telco closets. The individual buildings will be equipped with redundant fiber optic cable runs to ensure maximum uptime connected through business-class routers such as those available from Cisco Systems, Nortel, or the like.

Workstations

The existing workstations will not be retired but will be upgraded to ensure reliable operation. Their memory and hard drives will be upgraded to accommodate the latest Microsoft operating system. The existing 10 Mbps NICs will be replaced with 10/100 Mpbs NICs to provide more performance for RBSD now and in the near future. We recommend that a proprietary or name-brand server be purchased to add file sharing and printer sharing. Additionally, we recommend that Microsoft operating systems such as Windows XP Professional be installed on the workstations and the server for better interoperability, ease of use, and amount of compatibility.

CPU's Network

9

Learning Objectives

- Determine the business needs of Computer Professionals Unlimited, Inc.

- Given the business needs of Computer Professionals Unlimited, Inc., develop an appropriate network design.

Why Is This Chapter Important to Me?

Whereas the other two case studies have been client organizations, this case study will develop the network of our own company, CPU. Now our money, provided by the profit from our labor, will determine the structure of the network. The impartial and often easy decisions of a consultant who is not affiliated with an organization are not present in this environment.

The Basic Facts

As a recap of CPU's basic business conditions, the company was started as an extension of a class project while the principals were in college. They have tried to keep their business practices and customer relationships as professional but warm as possible. On the surface this may seem like a contradiction, but CPU has been able to walk that fine line between "friends" and "business associates." CPU is interested in long-term business relationships instead of short-term profits. As an added complexity, CPU has at least two different physical and logical networks at any time. One is the permanent CPU network, and the others are experimental networks for configuring customer equipment or testing theories.

Physical Location (See Figure 9.1)

CPU is located in a typical office space without a storefront. Because the company does not advertise and does not work with walk-in traffic, there is no need for a retail store. Because of CPU's rather small "footprint," the only unusual requirements are (1) there must be clean power that's reliable, (2) multiple broadband Internet accounts must be available, and (3) there must be the ability to floor-mount the rack equipment. Other than these requirements, CPU could exist in virtually any commercial office space or even a clean warehouse.

It's not absolutely necessary to floor-mount the racks. Because of their small size and the relatively small amount of networking hardware, it would be possible to use wall-mount or even tabletop racks instead. This may work, but it's not advisable for a variety of reasons:

1. Depending on building and electrical codes, an equipment rack may have to be floor-mounted or bolted to the floor. This could be for earthquake safety, electrical grounding, or other municipal codes.

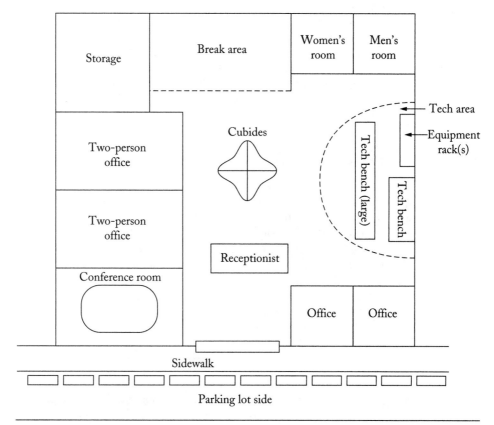

FIGURE 9.1 ◆ Office Plan (Hand Drawn)

2. A floor-mounted rack is more open and easier to reconfigure, troubleshoot, and see how the cables are connected with the equipment.

3. A floor-mounted rack gives potential customers a more professional display of how your network is built and installed.

Our Audience/Our Customer

Just as before, we need to understand the dynamics of the organization before recommending products, services, and configurations. This lesson was valuable with other companies, but it's just as important when trying to sell our own company something that we didn't know was obsolete, doesn't work properly and needs replacing, or is something new that the IT staff would like to try. Unlike our previous audiences, our company is much more attuned to technology in general, as well as its value to profitability. It should be easier to get organizational approval.

The principals of CPU are college buddies who decided to start this business out of a class project. They are fairly young. As such, they are looking for the long-term success of their business as a positive return on their investment as opposed to short-term profits. CPU is also run by techies who understand the value of choosing the right technology and using it wisely. Although it may sound contradictory to the last statement, CPU is frugal with purchases. Without a defined business need, nothing gets purchased!

Personnel

CPU's personnel have been grouped into support staff, consultants, and contractors. The duties of the support staff are office manager, accountant, personnel manager, and so on. The consultants also have specific duties: Web site design, network design, network administration, and the like. Certain contracts require more workers than CPU has on full-time permanent status. In such a case many consultants are ready to be called into action. These are mostly college students, network technicians needing extra income, and a variety of others. They must be given access to the company and customer computers, but this has always been in a limited capacity.

Summary

The network of CPU varies significantly from that of CCC and RBSD because of the nature of the organizations' needs and legacy equipment. CPU has a profit model for conducting its business, unlike RBSD. Every purchase must have a defined business need. The company has two separate networks: one for its own staff and one for any test equipment or client components.

Discussion Questions

1. Using the CPU network inventory spreadsheet from the Student CD, determine how much the network and all attached components would cost.

2. Would there be any advantage to leasing some equipment instead of purchasing it? If so, which devices or components would support the best arguments for leasing?

3. If you were given the task of deciding the network design, how would your final design differ from that of CPU?

4. Could you design a network that would address the normal staff, the experimental network, and the contractors' needs for $15,000? $20,000? $25,000?

Documents

Document 1   CPU BTA

◆ ◆ ◆

Business Needs

Computer Professionals Unlimited, Inc., is a relatively small computer and network consulting firm that specializes in providing the finest consulting and services possible. CPU does not have an inventory because components are purchased only after project bids have been accepted. The relatively few consultants and support staff help the company to be relatively lean but also to temporarily grow based on current business conditions.

Applications: Needed or Existing

CPU needs relatively few applications to perform its business operations. Its business productivity needs are accomplished via an office productivity suite such as Microsoft Office, Lotus SmartSuite, Sun Microsystem's StarOffice, or its freeware cousin OpenOffice. The financial tasks and analyses can be accomplished by using Intuit's Quickbooks Pro, MYOB, PeachTree, or another equivalent program. Each workstation should have a minimum set of system utilities such as antivirus, antispyware, and firewall software.

The consultants have specialized tools that exceed the minimum workstation software. CPU's Web site is designed and maintained using an HTML editor such as Microsoft's FrontPage, Macromedia DreamWeaver MX, or Website Pro's NetObjects Fusion. Network performance analysis is provided by software such as HP's OpenView, IP Switch's What'sUP Gold, or Agilent's Advisor. Although there are many network drawing programs, none is as inexpensive, easy to use, or compatible with Microsoft Office as Microsoft's Visio. Asset management or inventory can be accomplished through many of the same tools used for network analysis as long as there is a built-in SNMP functionality.

The server-associated tasks are provided by a network operating system such as Microsoft Windows, Novell NetWare, or UNIX/Linux. These include file and printer sharing, centralized data storage, Web serving, e-mail serving, and so on. Although any of the major network operating systems provide the required functionalities, the market dominance of Microsoft products almost requires that CPU use Microsoft Windows Server as its NOS.

Data/Traffic Characteristics: Office Network

Most network traffic consists of file and print sharing, accessing e-mail, Internet surfing, and instant messaging. Network traffic is expected to be unsustained peaks or bursts of activity.

Data/Traffic Characteristics: Experimental Network

Most network traffic consists of file and print sharing, accessing e-mail, Internet surfing, and instant messaging. Network traffic is expected to be unsustained peaks or bursts of activity. Due to the nature of the experimental network environment, there will be relatively little network traffic to monitor or design for.

Network Architecture: Office Network

After carefully weighing the options, we recommend that the network should be designed around the IEEE 802.3u or Fast Ethernet standard using Cat5e cabling. Each workstation should have standard 10/100 Mbps NICs connected with Cat5e cabling to Layer 2 switches—one for the support staff and one for the consultants. Because of this segmentation the network will have the capacity for higher bandwidth and the ability to isolate the different parts of the network for effective network troubleshooting. The network server should be equipped with two NICs to serve as a router between the two networks. This will allow both networks to function independently but still have server access, regardless of the configuration. Broadband Internet access will be provided by the Internet service provider that provides the greatest amount of bandwidth for the lowest cost.

Network Architecture: Experimental Network

The experimental network should reflect the overall characteristics of the majority of the customers' networks. As such, the network will be designed around an IEEE 802.3u or Fast Ethernet standard using Cat5e cabling. The network will have permanent Layer 2 workgroup switches connected to the same ISP as the regular office network but with its own individual account. This allows the networks to be connected through the public Internet in a real-world type of installation.

Technology Available

Cabling and Media

Beginning with the physical layer, the network cabling will be Cat5e UTP installed through the wall and terminated in standard RJ-45 wall sockets using the EIA/TIA 576B wiring standard. The cables will be terminated in the back of CPU's office to one or more patch panels in a standard floor-mounted network equipment rack with good cable management components.

Internet Access

Due to the absolute dependence on the public Internet for the proper functioning of CPU's network and its unique experimental or test network, it is recommended that CPU use a SOHO-class broadband connection (DSL or digital cable access) for each of the two separate networks. If the local service provider has uptime of less than 99%, we recommend an additional account, if another provider has the capacity and distribution, from another service provider. The basis for evaluating and choosing a broadband service provider is a combination of bandwidth versus cost and the guaranteed uptime and past resolution times.

Network Devices

The several network switches should be Layer 2 workgroup switches. The majority of them should be rack mountable; a few spare switches can be cheaper and lack the ability to be rack mounted.

Workstations: Support Staff

Because the support staff's workstation functions are standard, the workstations can be normal or proprietary systems with mostly standard equipment such as Pentium 4 or P4-class processors, 512 MB or more of RAM, 120 GB or larger hard drives, CDRW/DVD drives, Windows XP Pro, Microsoft Office 2003, Intuit's QuickBooks Pro (for financial tasks), and 17- or 19-inch LCD screens.

Workstations: Consultants

Although the consultants' workstations should be mostly similar to those of the support staff, the consultants require specific capabilities and applications to perform their jobs. Each system will require an upgrade of 1 GB or more of RAM and a CDRW/DVD-R/DVD-ROM drive. Specialized software is also required:

Specialized Task	Specialized Software
Website creation	NetObjects Fusion
Network documentation	Microsoft Visio
Packet analysis	IP Switch's What'sUp Gold

Server

CPU's office server should be a rack-mounted unit equipped with interchangeable hard drives (used both for disaster recovery and for multiple configurations) and an appropriate storage device such as a tape drive or CDRW/DVD-R unit. This server should be nonproprietary (otherwise known as a "clone" or Wintel system). The server should have 2 GB of RAM, 100 GB of hard drive storage, multiple 10/100 Mbps NICs, and Microsoft Windows 2003 Server (not Small Business Center 2003).

PART III

What Happens Next?

10

Performing the Installation

Learning Objectives

◆ Be able to develop an appropriate naming standard for network locations.

◆ Become proficient with the tools of the trade.

◆ Be able to efficiently plan cable installation, termination, and labeling.

◆ Be able to test a network after installation.

Why Is This Chapter Important to Me?

This chapter will help you in the real-world job market. Practical experience is what separates those who say they know how to do a task and those who actually know how to do it! Coursework, seminars, and certifications are all valuable tools, but practical experience is the deciding factor on the job.

Nomenclature, Naming, and Other Things

One of the most overlooked tasks within a wiring (or any other IT) project is the establishment of naming conventions or *nomenclature*. Simply put, nomenclature is the naming standard used, along with your network diagram, to identify the location of components, network jacks, and the like. Some organizations use their city and state addresses, room numbers, or proprietary or coded location names. Make these names unique and somewhat descriptive while being vague enough to foil the attempts of hackers to find out too much information about your network. If Company X has several U.S. locations, its nomenclature could easily be broken into city and state names, branch office locations, room numbers, and so on—for example, "KCMOBS112A" for Kansas City, Missouri, Blue Springs branch, room 112, first computer. The technician should be able to look at a network diagram and find location KCMOBS112A. It's a great idea to uniquely name and label each cable run as well. There should also be a cross-referenced or cross-linked file with the system inventory and its recent hardware and software changes. This will help the technician figure out any issue.

When naming your network locations, make each location name unique. Labeling the individual wires and jack locations with permanent marks or some sort of ID tape will help minimize errors.

The Tools

The contents of your toolkit can make carrying it around either a burden or a blessing. There's an important balance between having too much stuff and not enough, and you never really know until you're already at the job site. Although many technician toolkits are commercially available, there is no such thing as the ideal or perfect toolkit. At best there is a standard set of tools that has been personalized by the preferences of the technician and the typical working environment the technician experiences. For instance, a bench technician wouldn't need portable tools or a carrying case like a field technician.

FIGURE 10.1 ◆ Student Backpack

The author's preference is to use either a soft-sided tool kit or a backpack instead of a hard plastic or metal tool kit. It is easy to find an inexpensive, usable, and professional-looking backpack (see Figure 10.1) or messenger bag (see Figure 10.2) in discount outlets. These can be purchased in a variety of sizes, colors, and pocket arrangements. The main storage compartments of the pack can be customized with the addition of divided plastic storage boxes (see Figure 10.3). These boxes (roughly 12 × 6 × 2 inches with multiple compartments) are inexpensive and handy for carrying assorted screws, spare jumpers, zip ties, and electrical tape (see Figure 10.4). This type of tool kit is comfortable to carry, cost-effective, and adaptable to the ever-changing work environment.

A variety of standard tools should be in every toolkit. These include standard telco (RJ-45 and RJ-11) crimpers (see Figure 10.5) for terminating standard analog telephone and Cat5-type cabling. It might also be a good idea to invest a few dollars in a wire stripper and a set of diagonal cutters, also know as "dikes" (see Figure 10.6) or lineman pliers (see Figure 10.7). An alternative to the diagonal

FIGURE 10.2 ◆ Messenger Bag

FIGURE 10.3 ◆ Plastic Storage Box

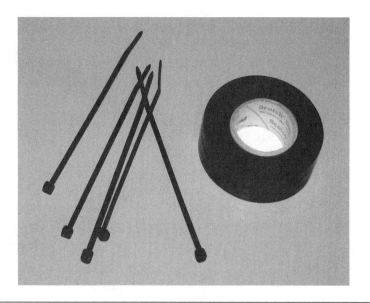

FIGURE 10.4 ◆ Zip Ties and Electrical Tape

cutters or lineman pliers is a multitool, such as the Gerber Multi-Pliers™ (see Figure 10.8). These work wonderfully and carry a lifetime guarantee against breakage. It's also advisable to have a multibit screwdriver (see Figure 10.9) instead of dozens of screwdrivers, nut drivers, hex key bit drivers, and the like to accommodate the variety of screws you'll encounter in the field. Of course, you

FIGURE 10.5 ◆ Crimper

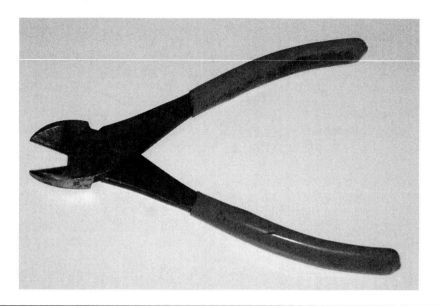

FIGURE 10.6 ◆ Diagonal Cutters

can always purchase a commercially available technician kit (see Figure 10.10), but the author thinks they are somewhat pricey, have substandard-quality tools, and either need other tools added to them or have way too many tools in them. It would probably be helpful to put a stud sensor (see Figure 10.11) and a drywall

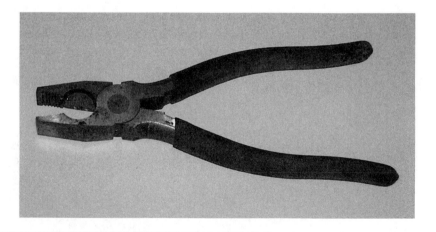

FIGURE 10.7 ◆ Lineman Pliers

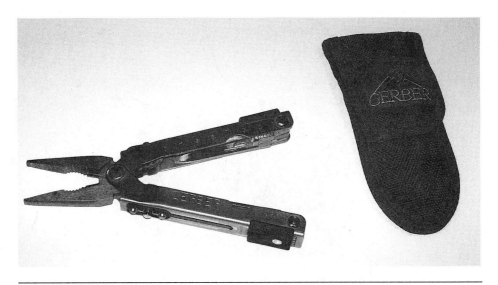

FIGURE 10.8 ◆ Gerber Multitool

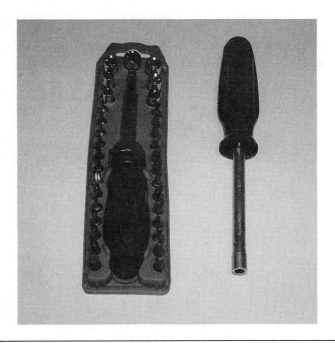

FIGURE 10.9 ◆ Multibit Screwdriver

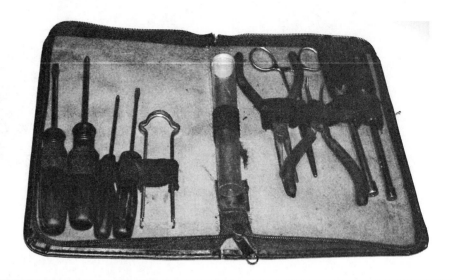

FIGURE 10.10 ◆ Commercial Kit

FIGURE 10.11 ◆ Stud Sensor

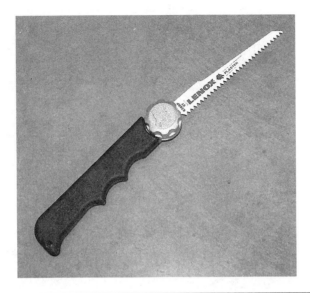

FIGURE 10.12 ◆ Drywall Saw

saw (see Figure 10.12) into your toolkit as well. There's nothing quite like trying to install an electrical box (see Figure 10.13), missing the support stud completely, and having to cut another hole, plus patch the hole you just made!

After installing your cabling, you'll need to test it. The simplest and cheapest tool (see Figure 10.14) just tests the electrical continuity of the network cabling. If a connection has been made, the cable will test correctly. If not there will be a short, which means that packets cannot be transmitted across the network. More expensive testers (see Figure 10.15) have additional capabilities beyond just testing the electrical or Layer 1 continuity. These can range in price from $250 to more than $10,000, and you get what you pay for. The more expensive testers, such as the Fluke OneTouch Series II Network Analyst (approximate cost $3,500), can map the network, certify the network cabling according to IEEE standards, ping remote devices, and so on. These are definitely the most elegant network testers, but it's difficult for a small or medium-sized company to justify their cost, unless your business is networking consulting and installation.

The author has included on the Student CD a Microsoft Excel spreadsheet with the contents of his toolkit, complete with approximate prices. It's not an exhaustive shopping list, but it's enough to get you started.

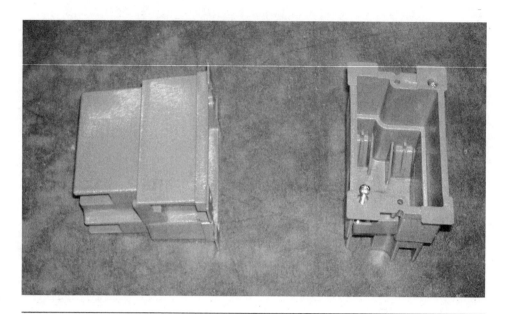

FIGURE 10.13 ◆ Electrical Box

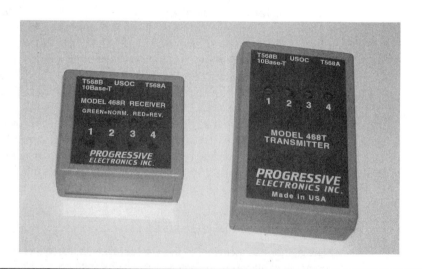

FIGURE 10.14 ◆ Cat5 Tester

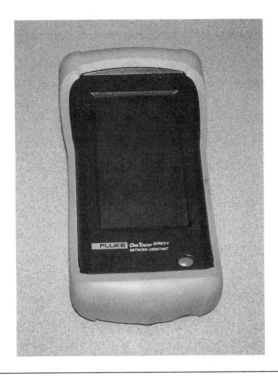

FIGURE 10.15 ◆ Cat5 Tester: Expensive

Installing Network Cable

"Pulling Cable"—During Construction

Perhaps the most tiresome and frustrating task is the actual installation of cabling within building infrastructure. The easiest type of installation is during building construction before the wall facing or drywall has been installed. In such a case the whole project can be completed with relative ease and speed. Here are the basic procedures:

1. Determine the best and most efficient path for each cable run.

2. Determine the lengths of cable needed (make sure to take into account the rise of the wall and all obstacles, as well as leaving slack for easy wire stripping and termination).

3. Cut 25% more cable than you *think* will be needed. (There is nothing more frustrating than to find out that you miscalculated the amount of wire and will have to repull an entire cable run!)

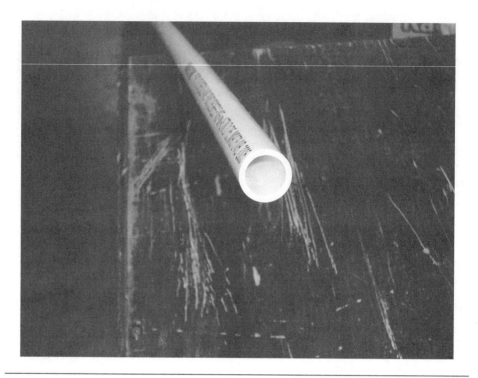

FIGURE 10.16 ◆ Wiring Conduit: Plenum

4. Install PVC or metal conduit (see Figure 10.16) if the project budget allows for it. If the budget doesn't allow this, run the numbers again and beg if you have to. (The cost of ¼-inch PVC water pipe or conduit is mere pennies per foot. This allows for the easiest wire pulling imaginable and also helps protect the cabling from damage after installation.)

5. If conduit is not possible, you will need to attach the cable to the bare studs with a little bit of slack (check with the manufacturer and municipal codes). Remember the extra 25% for any miscalculations and for cable length changes due to temperature.

6. Install your electrical boxes on the studs.

7. Run your cables from the network closet to the electrical boxes.

8. Terminate your cables as described next and in Appendix C.

9. To tidy up the installation you may need to use wire racks in the ceilings. These aid in the finished look of the cabling (for the customer) and in troubleshooting and maintenance (for the technician).

10. If a wall socket cannot be located close enough to a user's computer, you may wish to install exterior (to the wall) cable management or wire raceways, which can be attached either with double-sided tape or by screwing them onto the wall surface.

"Pulling Cable"—After Construction

If you were not fortunate enough to install the network during the construction phase, the task becomes *much* more difficult. In fact, you will most likely need one more piece of equipment in your tool kit: a fish tape. This will be used to *pull* the cable through holes cut into the wall for access. The same basic set of instructions is included here for comparison, with the differences noted:

1. Determine the best and most efficient path for each cable run.
2. Determine the lengths of cable needed.
3. Cut 25% more cable than you *think* will be needed.
4. *Install PVC or metal conduit (see Figure 10.16) if the project budget allows for it. If the budget doesn't allow this, run the numbers again and beg if you have to. (The cost of ¼-inch PVC water pipe or conduit is mere pennies per foot. This allows for the easiest wire pulling imaginable and also helps to protect the cabling from damage after installation.)* This step cannot be performed.
5. *If conduit is not possible, you will need to attach the cable to the bare studs, with a little bit of added slack (check with the manufacture and municipal codes). Remember the extra 25% for any miscalculations and cable length changes due to temperature.* This step cannot be performed.
6. *Install your electrical boxes on the studs.* This step can be performed with some slight modifications. Instead of installing the electrical boxes, you'll need to purchase in-the-wall brackets for mounting the wall plates without electrical boxes.
7. Run your cables from the network closet to the wall plates.
8. Terminate your cables as described next and in Appendix C.
9. To tidy up the installation, you may need to use wire racks in the ceilings.
10. If a wall socket cannot be located close enough to a user's computer, you may wish to install exterior (to the wall) cable management or wire raceways.

The author has seen many ways to run wire between locations. Fish tapes are difficult to use. The basic design of a fish tape is to take a piece of thin spring steel and coil it inside a plastic holder that can feed the tape out. The tape or steel is pushed through a conduit or wall space to the other end. Because the steel is a spring, it tends to bend or coil behind the drywall as well! A creative and fun method is to use a remote-controlled toy vehicle with wire attached. Another installer's idea was to use a cross-bow to pull the cable from one end of a building to another! Most technicians use the more traditional method of a "pull string": a thin rope that is put into place and then used to pull the network cabling from the box to the desired location.

Terminating Network Cable

Terminating network cabling is difficult to master. Some people find it more difficult to understand the physical aspects of network cabling than the more conceptual aspects such as network administration. It seems that every network technician has a different technique for terminating network cabling! Some of the most rational technicians have the most superstitious tips for success. In this text we will not discuss terminating fiber optic cabling. Instead we will focus on the termination of twisted pair cabling. As a refresher, twisted pair cabling consists of multiple pairs of copper wires encased in a PVC sheath. These are typically color-coded for identification. (For a more complete instruction set, see Appendix C.) The steps for terminating UTP (STP is similar) are summarized here:

1. Cut to length.
2. Strip off the outer conductor (see Figure 10.17).
3. Isolate the four pairs into a "flower."
4. Determine the EIA/TIA wiring standard.
5. Straighten the individual wires.
6. Arrange the wires according to the EIA/TIA wiring standard and insert them into the terminator.
7. Insert the terminator into the crimper.
8. Squeeze!
9. Test.

Because RJ-45 terminators are for single-use permanent installation, if the cables don't test properly, even after resqueezing with the crimpers, you will need to cut off the terminator and start the process from the beginning. This can become somewhat pricey!

The process for "punching down" wall sockets is somewhat similar:

1. *Cut to length.*
2. *Strip off the outer conductor.*

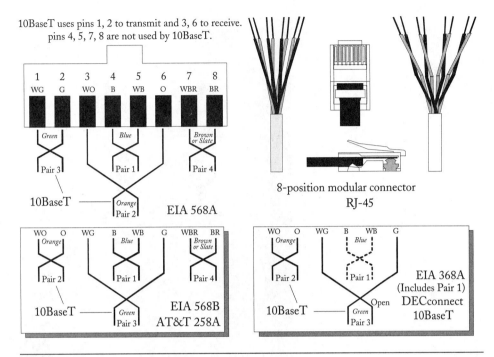

10BaseT uses pins 1, 2 to transmit and 3, 6 to receive. pins 4, 5, 7, 8 are not used by 10BaseT.

FIGURE 10.17 ◆ Twisted Pair Cable: Cat 5 or Cat5e (Cutaway View)

3. *Isolate the four pairs into a "flower."*

4. *Determine the EIA/TIA wiring standard.*

5. *Straighten the individual wires.**

6. *Arrange the wires according to the EIA/TIA wiring standard.*

7. Insert the wires into the color-coded termination points in the wall socket (see Figure 10.18).

8. "Punch down" with a 110 punch-down tool (see Figure 10.19).

9. Snap on wire covers to hold the wires in place.

10. Test.

---

*This is where techniques vary. The author prefers to grasp the unstripped portion of the cable between thumb and forefinger and the loose ends with the thumb and forefinger of his other hand. Then, with a bending motion followed by a rotating motion, the wires get straightened and cut straight across. The loose wires are inserted into the terminator or wall socket until you can see all eight copper conductors at the end of the terminator. (Without seeing all the conductors, you will not

FIGURE 10.18 ◆ Ethernet (RJ-45) Wall Socket: Back

get a good connection once the terminator is crimped.) Insert the terminator into the telco crimper and squeeze until the handles give a little. If the cable doesn't test correctly, you can recrimp or resqueeze the terminators—a technique with more than a 50–50 chance of working.

Testing the Installed Cable

After the cable has been installed and terminated, it will have to be tested. Few cable installations have no issues! Depending on the tester being used, you may or may not get quantifiable results. Simple Layer 1 continuity testers (see Figure 10.14) verify only that the cable has electrical continuity. More complex testers such as the Fluke OneTouch Series II Network Assistant (see Figure 10.15) provide data that can be printed and given to the client.

Regardless of the type of data obtained during testing, the client should be given a copy. Typically these data are gathered and presented in a binder.

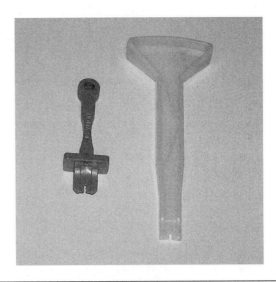

FIGURE 10.19 ◆ Disposable 110 Punch-Down Tool

This has two purposes. The installation company has written documentation that the network was installed correctly. And the client has verification that the entire network was tested and verified before the project was completed. (You will find a network verification template in Appendix E.)

Summary

This chapter introduced naming standards, which are extremely important to the installation, management, and troubleshooting of any network. The tools of the trade were also introduced—both those that are essential and those that are merely useful. The chapter also introduced the general process for installing network cabling, both before and after construction, and terminating the cable ends. Finally, you were introduced to basic network testing.

Discussion Questions

1. If you had only $75 to purchase network tools, what would be in your tool kit?

2. What unexpected problems could be found during a typical network installation?

3. A customer has just called complaining about Computer KSMOLS120N's connectivity to the network. Your technicians have just installed the cabling to that office location. How would you start the troubleshooting process?

4. Develop a naming standard for your school. Does the IT staff already have a naming standard? As a new network manager, would you change the naming standard and rename the components, or leave everything as it is?

11

Checking Network Health

Learning Objectives

- Become familiar with network analysis software and tools.
- Be able to justify the cost of network management software.
- Describe the importance of baseline measurements.
- Become familiar with packet analyzers or sniffers.
- Become familiar with SNMP-associated tools.

Why Is This Chapter Important to Me?

This chapter will expand on the skills presented in the previous chapters. To set the stage, we have designed and installed the network, but now we have to somehow check its health. Without a method for checking the health of a network, you'll never know if it's operating efficiently or correctly. Did you ever wonder if medical doctors forget what a healthy patient looks like because they see only sick patients? The same is true here. If there has been no network health assessment, how will you know if the network is "sick?" How will you be able to justify the next upgrade? The answers to these questions (and others) are vital to your career success and your job security.

How Do We Define Network Health?

For most of us this is tricky; but without a clear definition and quantifiable measures, network health can never really be assessed. The easiest way to determine what we need, or what is possible, may be to actually determine the "how" of the measurement and what a quantifiable measure might be. We'll start with a simple series of questions and responses:

End user:	"The network sure is slow today."
Network technician:	"Really? How slow is it?"
End user:	"Pretty slow. You know, slower than yesterday."
Network technician:	"If you had to put a number to it, what would it be?
End user:	"I don't think I can give a specific number, but it took a long time to boot up this morning."

You can see how frustrating this type of exchange can be to a network engineer. Without some hard data, there's no way to determine what the problem is or even how bad it may be.

Let's see how this exchange would look with some data:

End user:	"The network sure is slow today."
Network technician:	"Really? How slow is it?"
End user:	"Pretty slow. You know, slower than yesterday."
Network technician:	"If you had to put a number to it, what would it be?
End user:	"Normally it takes somewhere around 5 minutes to log on and check my e-mail, but today I've been trying to log on for the past 30 minutes.

This time we have some indication of the severity of the problem and what the user was trying to do when the issue became apparent. This is much more to go on! Without end users providing us with the information, how else can we obtain this type of documentation?

System and network monitoring can be handled in two different ways. The systems themselves can be monitored, either by proprietary software from the manufacturer or third-party software. The network itself can be measured by network packet analysis software or connectivity-probing software. Actually testing the network and not just the end user systems is more indicative of how the overall network is functioning, but we can't leave that part of the equation out either.

To explain how this works we'll have to digress into a brief discussion of telecommunications history. Electronic communications began as a series of ons (1s) and offs (0s). These bits (0s and 1s) were changed from digital to analog signals and transmitted through copper wiring from message beginning to message end without stopping. If there was a problem due to a downed communications line or a glitch somewhere, the entire transmission had to be resent. Not only was this time-consuming, but it was also bad for national security purposes. Imagine transmitting the data from a nuclear weapon test, and the transmission fails. Do you assume that there was just a problem in the wire, or do you assume that the enemy has compromised the transmission? This type of scenario happened routinely during the Cold War between the United States and the Soviet Union. The Department of Defense and the Department of Energy decided to invent some new technology, and thus the Internet was born. It has matured over a few decades and doesn't look anything like it did back then, but the Internet is a direct result of the fear of Cold War espionage.

The technological advance we're concerned with here is the advent of data being broken down into small, bit-sized pieces called "packets." Data packets could be sent independently of each other to the receiver's system. The transmission could also suffer some corruption without disturbing the whole message content. Let's examine a message composed of 2,512 kb being transmitted from Washington, D.C., to Seattle. In analog signaling the message could be corrupted at any point along the transmission without the knowledge of the sender or the receiver. The entire message would have to be retransmitted from beginning to end with little indication of where or when the transmission was damaged.

Since the advent of packet-switching networks (that is, since the introduction of the TCP/IP protocol suite), messages are broken into packets (or datagrams or frames) and then sent (sometimes independently) from the sender to the receiver. If part of the message is corrupted, either by loss of a transmission line or by some other means, only the damaged part needs to be resent. (The movie *Crimson Tide* is a great example of what the U.S. military did *not* want to happen! The basic story is that only part of a message is received about a nuclear attack. Before the entire message content is received to indicate what actions the nuclear submarine captain should take, the message is stopped.) Because of issues with transmission integrity, also called *nonrepudiation*, it is essential to have some sort of mechanism to determine how reliable the information is from sender to receiver. Another way to think of this is how spies use code words or phrases to verify that they're on the same side. As a result of this electronic "chatter" we can determine if the communicating parties are who they say they are; but more important to us, this system allows us to determine network health by the types and characteristics of communications.

There are no absolutes when it comes to how much and what type of communications are the optimal settings. The author has found many "experts" who purport to know the mysteries of network design. There are some rules of thumb but nothing that has been codified or otherwise officially endorsed. Until a network is physically installed there is no way to concretely determine overall network performance. This can be due to many factors such as electrical interference within the environment, different user behaviors, different automated network and server processes, quality of the network cabling, and others too numerous to mention here. There are some solid network simulation tools available that can help technicians determine a range of performance, but these can only provide an informed guess. The more information that can be input into the network simulation tool, the better the resulting predictions. The best way to provide this information is from an existing, real-time environment's actual network usage patterns. These are the network baselines mentioned before.

The Types of Tools

The standard tool for this type of analysis is packet capture or network analyzer software such as Microsoft's Network Monitor or Wild Packet's EtherPeek products. These work under the assumption that the basic network infrastructure or Layer 1 components are working properly. If there is not some sort of medium between two communications nodes, whether it is wireless, copper, twisted pair, or fiber, any software is useless! If there *is* a physical layer issue, a continuity tester is a more appropriate tool.

The basic parts of a network or packet analyzer are shown in Figure 11.1. You will need a network adapter or NIC attached to some sort of media (wireless works as well), and it needs to be put into "promiscuous mode." Promiscuous mode allows the NIC to listen to conversations destined for other NICs. The packet analyzer should also possess a capture filter, which acts like a video tape on a video surveillance system.

Packet capture software, commonly called "sniffers," can be obtained as open source freeware or commercially available products. These can also be written for specific operating systems such as Linux or UNIX-only products or Microsoft Windows–only products such as HP OpenView or EtherPeek. When it comes to sniffers, lower-cost or freeware products can be modified to provide the same level of analysis and functionality as the commercial products, but they may require substantial programming knowledge to be made useful for your specific environment and needs.

Typical functions include packet filtering or the gathering of packets based on preselected criteria, packet decoding or the breakdown of the packets into their data payloads and the encapsulating information, alarms or triggers that allow the sniffer to be preset to become active only when certain criteria are

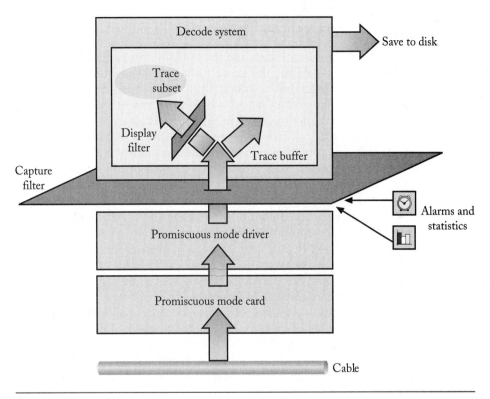

FIGURE 11.1 ♦ Network Analyzer Elements

met (think of this being like a motion sensor on an exterior porch light), and traffic statistics such as how many packets of what size were observed between 2:00 and 2:15 p.m. last Tuesday afternoon.

Although sniffers provide useful data for measuring overall network traffic, there is a significant downside. A principle in atomic physics states that you can know either where an electron is *or* how fast that electron is traveling. Werner Heisenberg developed this "uncertainty principle" when trying to accurately characterize electrons and their motion around their nuclei. This principle also applies to network analysis. In simplistic terms (this doesn't apply to every type of packet), a packet that is captured by the sniffer must be re-sent down the network. This traffic can add up to 30% extra traffic to the overall network usage. The trick becomes providing balance between monitoring the network too well, thus adding to the overall network traffic, and not gathering enough data to accurately determine the network's overall performance.

Performing the Analysis—Theoretically

If you're doing a baseline network health analysis, there are several issues to consider. Perhaps the most important issues are (1) having an overall view of network usage based on both location and the different user groups and (2) having a basic understanding of where and how the network is physically laid out. Without knowing how the network usage is distributed, you'll have no idea where the network traffic is generated. Without knowing how the network is laid out, you'll have no idea where to place your listening device. Network analyzer software works sort of like an eavesdropper on the specific segment of the network that it's attached to. If a network analyzer or sniffer were placed in the accounting department, it would be ineffective to determine the characteristics of the network traffic in the engineering department unless the entire network was connected with hubs. Layer 1 devices don't segment network traffic. Only Layer 2 and higher devices actually provide network segmentation or collision domains, thereby providing a more efficient traffic pattern for the network.

The first assessment of the network should probably be a weeklong baseline that gathers information continuously during a typical week (see Figure 11.2). This would provide a better understanding of daily network traffic so some correlations could be made. For instance, there should be a peak of network traffic at the beginning of each shift change, along with a corresponding peak as users are logging off at the end of each shift (see Figure 11.3). This type of analysis would prove almost useless if there was some sort of external increase or decrease of network traffic—such as the holiday shopping season for a retail organization.

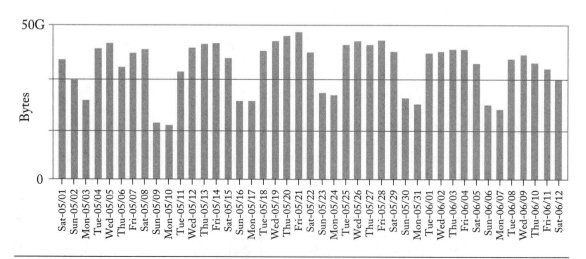

FIGURE 11.2 ◆ Baseline of Daily Network Traffic

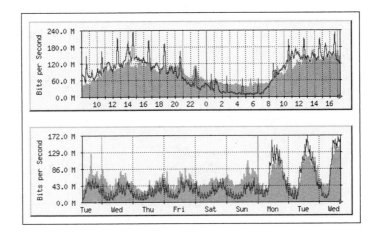

FIGURE 11.3 ◆ Graphs Generated by MRTG

Typical traffic patterns would be incomparable to those experienced during such times.

Some experts recommend that weeklong baselines be performed every quarter as sort of a routine "physical" for the network. Others recommend as little monitoring as once a year or not until there is a significant change within the organization. Depending on the amount of change within the network or the organization's personnel, either extreme might be appropriate; but the author tends to take a more balanced approach for most organizations. In a retail environment, at least two different standard baselines are appropriate: one for the typical network and one for the peak holiday shopping season. If there was significant growth, these should be performed at least annually, if not quarterly. Nothing hurts a retail organization more than having an outage during the holiday shopping season!

After the initial baseline, shorter and more focused monitoring should be based on observed user behaviors. For instance, most organizations have a large amount of e-mail and Internet traffic compared to other network operations. Although this traffic generally consumes only a small portion of the overall bandwidth, most users spend more time performing these operations than any other. Daily spikes of activity between 12:00 and 1:00 might justify investigating what behavior caused that traffic. It's probably something as mundane as online shopping, checking personal e-mail, or using instant messaging to communicate with friends and family. If traffic during that time were a hypothetical 25% of total bandwidth, concern would not be warranted unless there was an increase to double that amount. Such a traffic increase may be the first indication of some sort of network failure or even an attack, so a "trigger" in the sniffer program should be set to detect activity that is outside the baseline. Without an original baseline and subsequent focused monitoring, a network could be penetrated and used in some sort of an information attack.

Performing the Analysis—Hands-On

For this discussion the author downloaded a demonstration copy of WildPacket's EtherPeek software for Windows. Most network analyzers or sniffers provide the same types of functionalities and user interface.

After downloading and installing the EtherPeek product, you will be warned that this is demo software with limited capabilities. Before using a sniffer we'll have to do some configuration and customization. Typically the first configuration deals with selecting the adapter (see Figure 11.4). You may have more

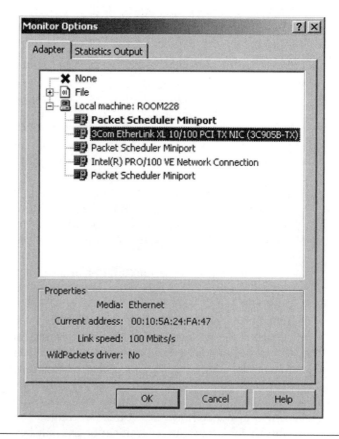

FIGURE 11.4 ◆ EtherPeek Screen: Adapter Select

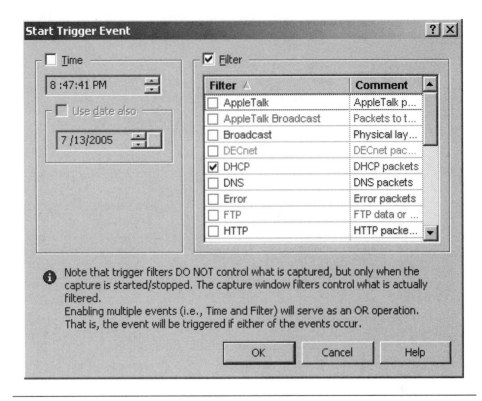

FIGURE 11.5 ◆ EtherPeek Screen: Trigger Event

adapters on your system than you thought. The next step is to determine if triggers will be set up (see Figure 11.5). Triggers are settings that begin capturing packets if a certain predefined action, circumstance, or characteristic is observed on the network, such as too much network utilization between 2:00 and 3:00 p.m. on Tuesday afternoons. It is also wise to configure filters that record only specific protocols or packets (see Figure 11.6). It can be frustrating to sort through thousands of packets when you're interested in only DNS processes, as seen in the figures. Most sniffers can also be configured to capture statistics at a predefined time and then save the reports in a variety of formats such as HTML or XML (see Figure 11.7). At this point your initial configuration is complete (as seen in Figure 11.8).

Once a capture has been sufficiently configured, named, and initiated, you will start seeing packets being received and recorded (see Figure 11.9). These packets form the basis of the network communication between the different and distinct nodes (or attachment points) that are within the same collision

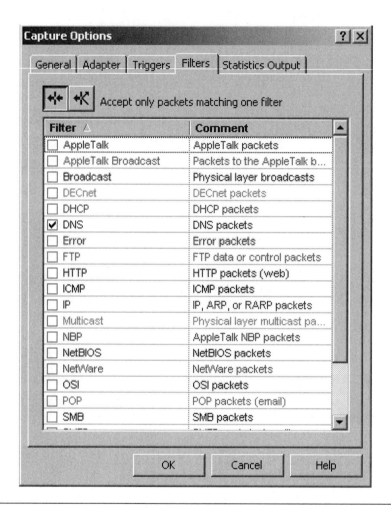

FIGURE 11.6 ◆ EtherPeek Screen: Filter Options

domain. These captures, or completed sniffs, can be manipulated in a variety of ways. The packets can be decoded so the contents can be viewed (see Figure 11.10). Additional analysis of the data can also be performed, such as an overall view of the network traffic (see Figure 11.11), a graphical view of the different nodes on the network involved in the communications (see Figure 11.12), an overall summary of the capture file (see Figure 11.13), saving options for the capture file (see Figure 11.7), and an "expert" analysis (see Figure 11.14) to help diagnose any problems such as malformed packets.

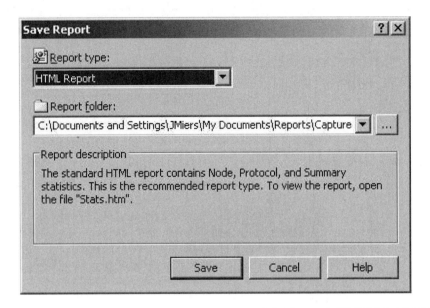

FIGURE 11.7 ♦ Packet Capture: Save Report

Although network/packet analyzers or sniffers are important and powerful tools for network technicians and engineers, they are an absolute treasure trove for anyone wanting inside information about the network. Active sniffers are almost impossible to detect because sniffers don't broadcast or send packets into the network. They only steal packets from the network, making them extremely difficult to detect.

Monitoring Systems

It might appear from our discussion that the only way to monitor a network is by monitoring the communication between systems. Although that is definitely one method, let's not forget about the sending and receiving systems on each end and the communications devices in between. The default TCP/IP protocol installation includes a little-known systems monitoring tool. It's called Simple Network Management Protocol (SNMP). Typically it has been turned off without user intervention, especially on Win 9x systems. It's actually a powerful conduit for shuffling information back and forth between monitored systems and the monitoring systems. There is one catch, though:

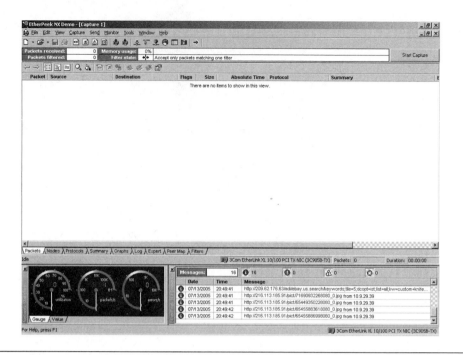

FIGURE 11.8 ◆ EtherPeek Screen: Main Screen

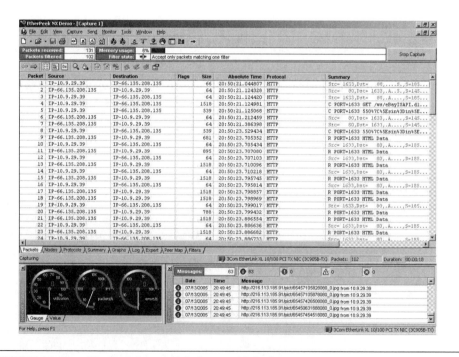

FIGURE 11.9 ◆ EtherPeek Screen: Main Screen with Packets

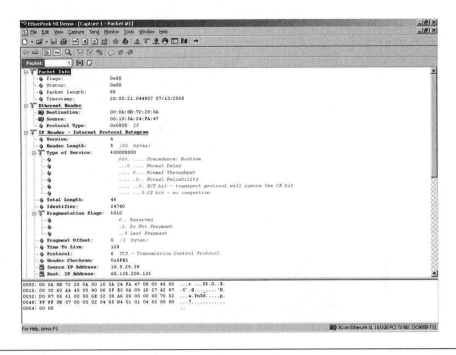

FIGURE 11.10 ◆ Packet Capture: Packet Decode

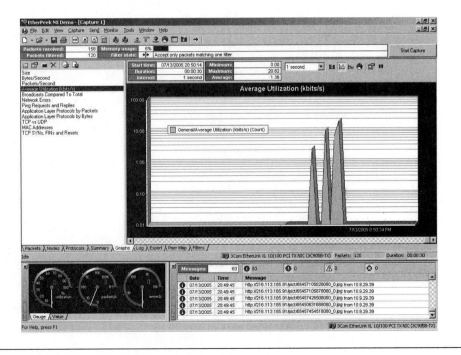

FIGURE 11.11 ◆ EtherPeek Capture: Network Utilization

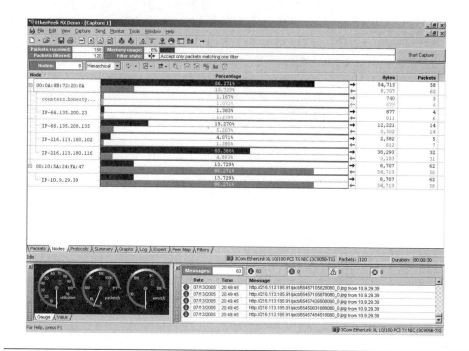

FIGURE 11.12 ◆ Packet Capture: Traffic between Nodes

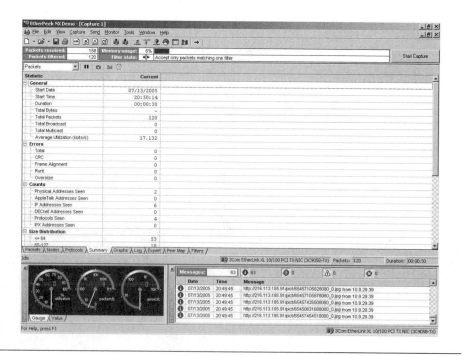

FIGURE 11.13 ◆ Packet Capture: Summary

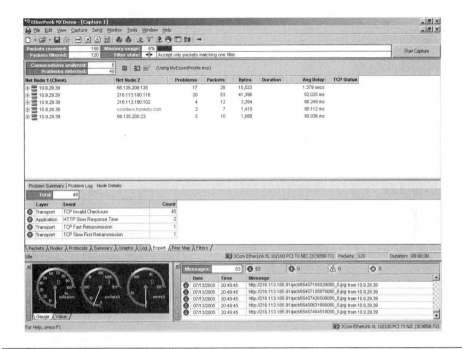

FIGURE 11.14 ◆ Packet Capture: "Expert" Advice

The protocol is distributed for free, but you'll have to obtain your own specific front-end application to use SNMP.

Most devices with functionality of Layer 2 or higher have to be programmed with a management information base (MIB). An MIB is a database that stores information about a system's capabilities and overall health. This MIB gathers information for a remote monitoring agent to retrieve. The information is ferried from the monitored system to the monitoring system using SNMP (see Figure 11.15). These data are collected and can be viewed by network monitoring software such as Microsoft Performance Monitor, Belarc Advisor, HP OpenView, or others. This provides the administrative front-end to SNMP's powerful capabilities.

For the network administrator, the capabilities of remote system monitoring and the implications of such monitoring are enormous. If a router is having issues in your branch office in Greece but no one is locally available to help, how will you resolve the issues? You could either hire a contractor to travel to this location or get on a plane and travel there yourself. This is an extreme example, but that's exactly what had to happen before the widespread implementation of SNMP. In some cases, such as secure government or military installations, that's still what happens—not because of SNMP but for security reasons.

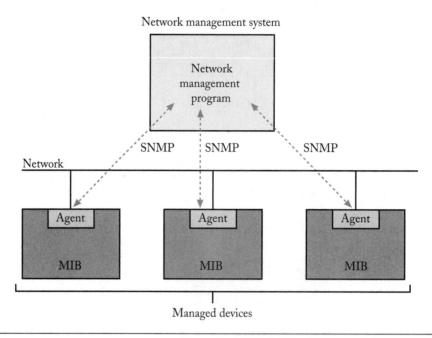

FIGURE 11.15 ◆ SNMP: Network Management Architecture

As before, we will be using a specific product, this time Belarc's Advisor, to illustrate the power of SNMP software. After the download and installation, Advisor will begin a scan of the local system (see Figure 11.16) that will take anywhere from 30 seconds to several minutes, depending on the number of

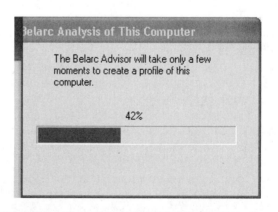

FIGURE 11.16 ◆ SNMP: Belarc Scan

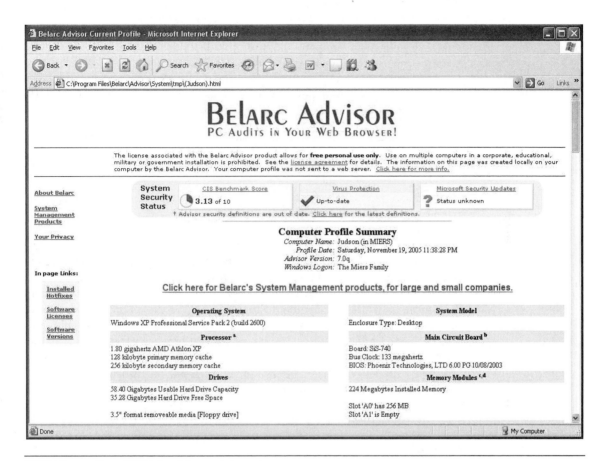

FIGURE 11.17 ◆ SNMP: Local System Information

devices and the system's performance. After completing the scan, Advisor will display the information it has gathered in a standard HTML format for viewing with IE, Firefox, Navigator, or some other Web browser (see Figure 11.17).

Although Belarc Advisor's demo software is being used on the local system, it illustrates the type of information that can be gained from SNMP software. In fact, Belarc's commercial version can gather the same information remotely.

The report shows that Advisor was able to gather hardware information as specific as the BIOS version and date, system serial numbers (if available), hard drive specifications and amount of data stored, printers that are attached, and so on. You can also see user accounts along with the last time users logged into the system, network connectivity, shared drives, and more. Not visible from Figure 11.17, Advisor even gathered the software information such as registration numbers, hot fixes and patches, and version numbers. Such tools could serve a dual purpose for both network monitoring and asset management!

Summary

After installing a network it's wise to monitor and manage the associated devices. These measurements can be reviewed with accuracy only when compared with a baseline analysis, which can also be used to justify future purchases. Baselines can be used for a variety of purposes, such as determining typical network usage, providing the standard to compare actual network usage with, and providing the justification for new purchases based on historic baselines.

TCP/IP comes bundled with a powerful network monitoring tool called SNMP (Simple Network Management Protocol). SNMP allows Layer 2 and above devices to be monitored remotely and automatically. If the network analyzers measure network traffic, SNMP analyses measure the network devices. Remote monitoring of systems, as facilitated by SNMP, is vital to even a medium-sized network and especially for multifloor, multibuilding, multilocation networks. Often these SNMP tools can be used for asset management as well.

Discussion Questions

1. Research three different network analyzers. Compare them by answering the following questions:
   a. What is the initial cost to obtain the product?
   b. Does this change if you would like to monitor 250 workstations?
   c. What features are most advertised with each product?
   d. What features are not present that you would like to have?
   e. What is your recommendation if the company had an unlimited budget?
   f. What is your recommendation if the company had little or no budget?
2. How would you deploy monitoring tools in your network? Just between nodes, just between subnets, or at each workstation? Defend your answer.
3. After establishing a network baseline, you see an increase from the first Tuesday shown to the next Monday. Would this concern you? What could be possible explanations for this increase?

4. Visit the following Web site and download a trial version of Belarc Advisor (www.belarc.com) for use with this question. Download it to your local workstation, install it, and run an inventory. Print out your results.

5. Open your workstation's Device Manager and print the results of that information. Compare the printouts obtained here and in Question 4.

6. How useful would this type of information be if your organization had remote locations in out-of-the-way places or even other countries?

12

Planning the Next Upgrade

Learning Objectives

- Understand the importance of seeing the network as a work in progress.
- Be able to identify the upgrade mechanism for your organization.
- Be able to justify the cost of the next planned upgrade.
- Be able to provide solid evidence to support your future purchases or leases.
- Understand the importance of the total cost of ownership to the overall budgetary process.
- Become familiar with the purchase versus lease debate.

Why Is This Chapter Important to Me?

So far we've spent our time exploring how a network functions, learning how to install network components, and monitoring systems for performance. Shouldn't we be done at this point? Absolutely not! A network is as fluid as the business environment within which it exists. What works for the network today may be inadequate next year.

General Guidelines

Every piece of equipment has several costs associated with it. There are the initial costs, the maintenance costs, the total cost of ownership (TCO), and its depreciation schedule. The TCO is the overall and complete cost of the item throughout its entire lifespan. Some equipment is fairly inexpensive to purchase but may cost much more with a maintenance contract, upgrade costs, training, and depreciation. Depreciation is a measure of the loss of value that a component experiences based on its expected lifespan. In simple terms, a company service van may have an expected lifespan of five years, and the annual cost associated with the van is roughly one-fifth of its original value. At the end of its "useful life," the value should equal zero.

The subject of depreciation is its own course for accountants. My explanations are simplistic, but the overall idea is that a component is lessened in value (or costed) by a predetermined amount that helps to offset its purchase price. This also helps to budget enough money for its replacement at the end of its useful life.

The network manager and accounting department must agree on the useful lifespan of each network device. This number will be used to set up the depreciation schedule for budgeting purposes. This is also a useful way to help lay the foundation for future upgrades.

Scheduled Upgrades

Some organizations use a predetermined schedule to perform their upgrades. During the "dot-com bubble" many companies upgraded their network equipment every two or three years. This was a time of both financial security and great technological innovation. It seemed that the release of new Microsoft Windows operating systems and Intel processors was coming at an unbelievable pace. If companies didn't have the latest technologies, they wouldn't have a competitive advantage. Companies with sufficient funding were scrambling to keep up with the "cutting edge." Those without sufficient funding felt inadequate and fearful of their competitors. Because of such philosophies and general market trends, many companies did not follow sound business practices and became overextended. On a brighter note, many companies were able to rework their business practices so that the cost of regularly upgrading their computers and networks became an accepted cost of business.

Automatic Upgrades Based on Performance

Some companies automatically upgrade their equipment when network performance levels reach a certain level. As an illustration, let's say that the company has a policy that the network will be upgraded if utilization reaches a level of 75% during nonpeak hours or if peak utilization is some multiple of the normal baseline.

"Adversarial Upgrades"

Many companies are adversarial about their network upgrades. The network manager must prove that the network has to be upgraded before any significant discussion can take place. The network staff may want more and better equipment, but the accounting staff is typically unwilling to release any funds to purchase new equipment. This is one of the best justifications for having performed a baseline performance measurement. A proper baseline should give ample evidence for the necessity of a network upgrade if the request is timed appropriately.

Building the Case

Justifying a network upgrade or expansion means explaining why additional funds are required after the network was installed or upgraded the last time. The argument from the business side of the organization is that much money has already been spent designing and purchasing the network equipment, installing the components, training users, and so on. The best way to counteract this argument is with facts.

Gathering information about the network and its performance is not exciting, but asset management (AM) and performance baselining are priorities. You should know how the network is working before you begin to change, modify, or upgrade it. Also, keep a journal of what you have done to the network. This should document passwords, network paths, custom configurations, and most important, what you have done to a particular system.

Many techies feel that the only way to have a measure of job security is to keep secrets. They fear that good documentation may make it easy to replace them with someone else who doesn't require as much salary. Although this may true in a few organizations, few managers are impressed by a "cowboy" who doesn't have any formal documentation and organizational skills. If there is no documentation, some people think they'll be able to extort more money and authority from their superiors. This may work for a few companies for a short time, but many will become frustrated and find a replacement faster than if the technician had worked as a part of the team. It's also unlikely that you'll want to spend your entire career at the same organization in the same position. This means you'll be looking to change positions and will want a good reference instead of having the reputation of being a renegade who doesn't "play well with others!"

Asset management is essential because you need to know what has already been purchased, if and how it's being used, and if it's even still on the premises. I've found that many organizations purchase components with good intentions and then never actually implement them, only to find they're no longer present when someone searches for them later. AM is also useful for determining how much the organization has spent previously, the approximate age of the components, and the overall view of the specific network components. You'll have to work with the accounting department to generate accurate monetary figures for these findings.

Performance baselines show how the network is functioning in its typical unaltered state. It's difficult to overstate the importance of this. If network utilization is at 75% (nonpeak), and you invest in a managed Layer 3 switch and network utilization goes down to 30%, you've just provided the cost–benefit justification for that expenditure. This gives concrete data for justifying this purchase and possibly the next upgrade as well. Such data are also useful for salary negotiations or for justifying more funding. If you can prove that the network is running more smoothly and this can be coupled with an increase of financial gains for the organization with a small price tag, you'll win that argument every time! It is also beneficial, although rare, for a company to have a cost–benefit contract. For instance, for every $1,000 of new purchases you may have to lessen network utilization by 5%, and if there is no reasonable expectation of that being accomplished, the organization may not proceed with the upgrade.

Network Simulations

Although this topic is largely out of the scope of this text, network simulation tools are wonderful ways to design your networks. However, network simulation tools such as OpNet, Agilent Advisor, and others are expensive and difficult to operate. In fact, there are courses and certifications just to use such programs.

These programs use statistical models and data to determine how network traffic will be distributed and characterized. They work best with an existing network baseline so the numbers are more realistic. They can be used with an initial design as well, but they excel with the data from an existing network.

The results of network simulations can be validated by electronically designing your existing network and comparing the expected performance with the actual performance from the baselines. You may have to reconfigure your network simulation so the analyses are more consistent. This will serve as validation that the new network you've envisioned will perform adequately before the company lays out funds. This should also help bring the accountants on board because of the demonstrable findings.

Total Cost of Ownership

The last topic we will explore in this chapter is that of TCO or total cost of ownership. Without being overly vague, there are costs associated with an item other than its initial purchase. Let's use a couple of components as an example:

	Component 1	Component 2
Initial purchase	$500	$350
Expected lifespan (in years)	3	5
Annual maintenance contract	$150	$175
Initial training	N/C	$75
Total cost of ownership	**$950**	**$1,300**

It's clear from this example that the TCO for Component 2 is much higher than for Component 1. If all things are equal except for the cost, which component would you pick? Although Component 2 has a longer expected lifespan, most companies would probably pick Component 1.

The author's grandfather knew the value of good equipment. He learned of a man named Bo Randall who made knives in Orlando, Florida. For those who aren't familiar with handmade knives, Randall knives are the finest knives made in any country. They formed a relationship, and eventually he bought one each of Randall's 13 models with stag handles.

The original price of those knives, if purchased today, would be $350 (average) × 13 = $4,500 or so. That's a tremendous price to pay for some fishing and hunting knives, except all of those knives are still used every hunting season over 40 years later. If you determine the TCO for those knives, the annual cost (if they lasted only 40 years) would be under $9 per year.

Another factor to consider is "purchase versus lease". Historically, companies had to purchase their equipment, depreciate it, and then find some place for it when it had outlived its useful life. Now there is the option to lease components, which can be attractive. Not only are there tax savings and simplifying of accounting procedures, but there is also the fact that the equipment can be upgraded at the end of a lease. The major downside to leasing is the finance fee. This is effectively the same as purchasing the equipment using credit. Buying computer equipment on credit is like purchasing fresh fruit on credit. Both computers and fresh fruit are worth more today than they will be tomorrow, and buying them on credit means you have to purchase them for full price plus interest on an asset that is rapidly decreasing in fair market value.

	Purchasing	**Leasing**
Advantages	Actually own equipment. Equipment becomes asset. Equipment can be used however company wants.	Tax savings. Equipment is not an asset. Equipment can be easily replaced at end of lease.
Disadvantages	Equipment loses value. Stuck with equipment after useful life is over.	Don't own equipment. Equipment is not an asset. Equipment use has limitations.

As a guideline, many organizations purchase their desktop systems and network servers because they feel that there is something inherently advantageous about owning the equipment you use most. Typically, companies will lease or even rent their "overflow" systems (systems that may be needed for a temporary increase in headcount) and their "high-availability" network infrastructure such as their routers. These devices are typically very costly, require much configuration and maintenance, and require technical support from highly certified individuals usually not found in small or medium-sized companies.

Summary

When it is time to upgrade your existing network, the same design guidelines apply as before. You will follow the same overall process for designing the technical aspects of the network except that the overall characteristics of the network have changed. The most important parts of the process are asset management (AM) and performance baselining. These help determine the exact state of the network both historically and currently and help build the case for upgrades or expansion of the network. The AM will also help to determine exactly what is on the network. This will most likely have to be performed in conjunction with the accounting department.

There are several mechanisms by which companies upgrade their equipment. Some companies have an automatic process by which, after certain criteria have been achieved, the network is upgraded; some companies have a more adversarial approach that requires justifying the upgrade and how much will be upgraded. Justifying your network upgrades may be more difficult than you think. That's why we use the AM and performance baselines as our main justifications for any upgrades. Another useful piece of evidence is a network simulation tool such as OpNet or Agilent Advisor.

Discussion Questions

1. Develop a template for the network journal that each technician should be keeping.
2. Evaluate two or three network simulation tools to determine which would be the overall best choice for your network infrastructure.
3. Playing the part of the accounting department, what types of evidence would you require before spending the company's funds?
4. Your boss has just asked you to prepare a presentation outlining the differences between buying and leasing. Whom would you contact for help with this presentation? What do you think would be the best answer for your company?

13

Evaluating and Choosing IT Employees, Consultants, and Service Providers

Learning Objectives

◆ Become familiar with various labor classifications.

◆ Become familiar with different types of IT professionals.

◆ Become familiar with various industry and/or vendor certifications currently available.

◆ Be able to develop selection criteria for evaluating potential vendors, IT professionals, and the like.

Why Is This Chapter Important to Me?

This text has used case studies to provide a more real-world learning environment for understanding network design. Along the way we've been introduced to some fundamental principles such as the OSI model, the top-down business model (or business and technology analysis or BTA), and some basic characteristics about networks and their components. We haven't delved into one topic that may be the most important: evaluating and choosing your IT staff! Choosing the right IT folks, whether they are employees or consultants or service providers, can be difficult and intimidating. Because of a recommendation of a consultant or group of consultants, your organization may become locked into a contract because of some proprietary or unusual component that only they are competent with! In short, choosing the right IT folks lets you concentrate on your business while they give you the tools (computers, networks, e-mail addresses, and so forth) that support the business.

Employees, Contractors, or Service Providers

Employees

Definition: Employees are individuals who rely on your organization for their primary paychecks or salaries.

By definition, employees are members of the organization they work in. In other words, their performance has a correlation with their paychecks. This isn't always the case, but in a perfect world, employees possess some sort of "ownership" or responsibility for the company within which they work. There is a measure of comfort in having on-site employees provide your IT services. Many believe it is better to use employees than contractors for these reasons:

1. Employees have more responsibility to make sure the job is done right.
2. Employees are inherently cheaper because they're already being paid by the company, even if the company has to pay for training.
3. Employees have more accountability to the organization and its management.
4. Employees can be trusted more.
5. If employees are used, the technical knowledge is within the company instead of with a contractor.

Contractors/Consultants

Definition: Contractors are individuals or companies hired to perform a narrowly defined task and then dismissed at the fulfillment of the contract.

Contractors do not work for your company. Either they work for themselves as individual consultants, or they work for a contracting agency. Contractors are generally more knowledgeable about specific and sometimes arcane technologies that are not well known to the general public. Contractors are also useful because the company has no implied relationship with them after the conclusion of the contract. There are some significant reasons why organizations choose contractors over employees:

1. Contractors typically possess specialized knowledge not known to most companies.
2. It's relatively easy to dismiss contractors after the completion of a task, or even before if they are not able to fulfill the contract.
3. Although contractors are initially more expensive, they are not entitled to company benefits.
4. Contractors can typically provide training for their products and services.
5. No one at the company can be blamed if the contractor messes up!

Service Providers

Definition: Service providers are a more extreme form of contractors. They actually become a for-hire IT department but work with your company through long-term relationships.

It is becoming more attractive and common to have part or even all of your IT functions contracted out through a service provider. Although service providers are technically contractors, they are usually retained on the basis of yearly or longer contracts. Service providers actually become your IT staff. In a perfect world, service providers can provide buying advice, strategic vision, and training. In short, service providers become the IT department you either never had or had to downsize because of its cost. Here are some of the reasons why companies choose service providers:

1. They offer one-stop shopping for IT services and sometimes products.
2. They provide the technical knowledge of contractors but offer more stability because of long-term relationships.
3. The relationship is almost like having your own IT staff.
4. The service provider gets the call in the middle of the night when the server goes down.

Evaluating Your IT Professionals: Education and Training
Self-Taught Individuals

The author admits that he is a largely "self-taught" individual (STI), and there's nothing wrong with this type of individual, per se. Many very qualified individuals are self-taught or learned through on-the-job training. Admittedly, STIs are a bit of a risk because there is little way to accurately judge their overall competence.

Recommendations: Shy away from STIs unless you have some way to test their knowledge, such as a skills-based test or practicum, written test developed specifically for the position and tasks they might be applying for, or certification through industry-standard testing bodies such as CompTIA, Microsoft, Novell, Cisco, or the like.

Vocational Technical Schools

Many high schools and local community colleges offer the benefit of semiformal or formal education without the high cost and extra courses required by traditional colleges and universities. Many individuals are trying to change careers, want to "test the waters" before investing a lot of time and money, or have discovered a particular interest in a specific type of IT career. Some of these facilities offer good training programs with focused education. Many of these are used to provide certification-type courses instead of a more broad-based college education.

Recommendations: If you're looking for career-focused training at a low cost, these types of school may be the best place for your time and energy. In hiring, look for individuals with certifications or completed coursework from schools that have a significant hands-on portion of their coursework.

Colleges and Universities

The value of a college education extends beyond the career field and in ways that cannot be measured in just financial terms. The education gained at a university is not only within a particular field of study, like the vo-tech or technical school, but seeks to develop a more rounded individual. But the technical education at a traditional university is not much different than that at a vo-tech or community college. Colleges and universities are better for lifelong learners who want to know the why and how. Individuals who have invested in a degree program tend to expect more than a technician's job as an overall career goal.

Recommendations: Look for individuals from schools known for the technical knowledge of their alumni and students. Also, make sure that their skills come not just from lecture courses but also from hands-on experience such as employment as a lab intern, tutoring of other students, attendance of professional organizations, and so on.

Certifications

Certifications hold promise for those who are new to the industry (without significant work experience in IT) or for individuals with specific job duties and tasks where the specific knowledge and benefits gained from being certified are justified.

Certifications are either industry-specific and therefore vendor-neutral or vendor-specific. Certifications can range from the basic ability to navigate the Web and send e-mail (I-net+ and Certified Internet Business Strategist) to the ability to configure the heart of the Internet (Cisco Certified Internetworking Expert) to anything in between. Individuals pursuing specific certifications can employ a number of strategies to gain specific knowledge, including self-study materials, overall industry knowledge, informative Web sites, official and unofficial courses, and so forth.

Certifications provide a number of specific benefits both for employer and employee or client and consultant:

1. Certifications demonstrate a minimum competence in a standard curriculum.

2. Certifications provide validation of the specific knowledge or skill that an individual has with a specific technology.

3. Many providers offer specific benefits on a "certified-only" basis such as lower-cost technical support, nonpublic information about product releases, career help, and the like.

Certifications cannot provide the saturation obtained from being in the industry for a number of years. They also test only the knowledge that the certification organization wants tested. As an example, you may know of a freeware product that would solve a complex and frustrating problem associated with Microsoft Windows XP Professional, but Microsoft's certification tests do not include third-party solutions. That's not to say that Microsoft or any other certification vendor is malevolent or lacking technical knowledge of these solutions; but there is no feasible way to assess all the different ways a particular problem can be solved. Also, it would look like the certifying organization had some sort of a partnership with this third-party company, which may not be true.

There is a significant downside to the proliferation of certifications: abuse. Passing the tests does not necessarily translate into technical competence. Some people have found ways to cheat on the tests by memorizing the test answers found on the Web. Such sites feature the recollections of individuals who have taken an exam and, on the way out, "dumped" what was in their short-term memories onto Web sites.

Beware, too, of the "awesome power of certification." After passing a certification exam, some people are so full of enthusiasm that it makes them cocky.

Recommendations: Certifications are good but not perfect measures of technical competence. Look for individuals who have both certifications and real-world experience or certifications and a college degree.

Common Certifications

A+ Certified Service Technician (www.comptia.org)
Developed by CompTIA, the A+ is an industry certification backed by a broad range of individual technology companies such as Intel, Apple, Microsoft, Novell,

Cisco, and others. The A+ is designed to measure the skills of someone who has been in the industry for over six months performing computer service and repair.

Recommendations: This is a good first certification and always a good benchmark for anyone working on computers, workstations, and servers.

Network+ Certified Network Technician (www.comptia.org)

The Network+ is another certification developed by CompTIA but specifically designed to test network technicians instead of computer technicians. Completion of this exam often qualifies individuals for cross-certifications in other certification tracks such as the MCSE or CNE.

Recommendations: This is a good second certification, after A+, for network technicians.

Certified Novell Administrator/CNA (www.novell.com)

Novell developed this certification over a decade ago to ensure the quality of their network administrators. This certification is considered the first test in the Certified Novell Engineer or CNE certification track.

Recommendations: This is a good first test for network administrators to learn a stable and straightforward network operating system.

Certified Novell Engineer/CNE (www.novell.com)

The CNE track is a series of certifications covering Novell's entire product line and job descriptions from NetWare administrator to GroupWise e-mail administrator to overall network engineer. Depending on the version of NetWare used, a person has to pass at least six tests before achieving the CNE certification.

Recommendations: This certification is useful only if your current or prospective company uses Novell NetWare products in their network infrastructure. There are few new installations of Novell NetWare. The need for CNEs is typically for existing installations at large organizations who have already implemented Novell's networking products.

Microsoft Certified Professional/MCP (www.microsoft.com)

Not to be outdone by Novell, Microsoft released its own certification track beginning with the Windows NT product release. By showing your proficiency with one of Microsoft's many products (except for the Microsoft Office product certifications called Microsoft Office User Specialist or MOUS) such as Windows XP Professional, Windows 2003 Server, Exchange Server, or the like, you can become an MCP.

Recommendations: This is a valuable certification because of the large number of Microsoft product installations. It's a good stepping-stone to MCSA or MCSE.

Microsoft Certified Server Administrator/MCSA (www.microsoft.com)

This certification is a fairly new one somewhere between the MCP and the MCSE. It requires more tests and therefore gives more financial power than the MCP but is not as rigorous as the MCSE. Consider this an interim certification on your way to the MCSE. It's sort of like getting an Associate of Arts degree on the way to a Bachelor of Science degree.

Recommendations: Consider this a stepping-stone to the MCSE. It provides leverage in job interviews; it's better to have completed a set of certifications than to have various certifications without being on a certification track.

Microsoft Certified Server Engineer/MCSE (www.microsoft.com)

The MCSE is the flagship of Microsoft certification. Much like Novell's CNE track, the MCSE has various options for specialization and indulging both professional and personal interests. There are a minimum of six individual certifications to achieve the MCSE.

Recommendations: This is an excellent certification because of the large number of Microsoft product installations. It offers good job security because of product brand recognition in industry HR departments.

Linux+ (www.comptia.org)

The Linux+ certification by CompTIA is an industry recognition that Linux is finally ready to be on center stage along with Novell and Microsoft. The Linux+ prepares the student for installing, administering, and troubleshooting the broad array of different versions of Linux that are in the marketplace today.

Recommendations: This is a very good entry-level certification to prove Linux competence. Because Linux installations grow daily, you should see a positive return on your investment here.

Red Hat Certified Engineer/RHCE (www.redhat.org)

Think of the RHCE as either the CNE for Novell or the MCSE for Microsoft. This is Red Hat's premiere certification to prove your technical skills with their version of Linux. With IBM's and Dell's installations of this OS on their products, look for the marketplace to demand the kind of skills the RHCE measures.

Recommendations: This is a good premiere certification for Linux experts. Expect excellent returns for this certification.

Certified Cisco Network Associate/CCNA (www.cisco.com)

The CCNA is the entry-level certification for working with Cisco switching and routing equipment. It is considered the foundation upon which the advanced Cisco certifications such as the CCIE are built.

Recommendations: This is a good certification if you are going to specialize in network infrastructure instead of the NOSes (CNE or MCSE). There are many Cisco installations to provide positive career advancement.

Cisco Certified Internetworking Expert/CCIE (www.cisco.com)

The CCIE is a coveted and valuable certification to achieve. Currently there are fewer than 20,000 CCIEs in the world. With a CCIE, you will have taken six or more written and skills-based exams at a Cisco testing facility to prove your worth. If you're excited by building and tuning the Internet, this is the certification for you!

Recommendations: This certification is costly, frustrating, and difficult to achieve. For those who achieve the CCIE, the career prospects and long-term financial outlook are great!

Summary

In this chapter we have explored some of the ways to evaluate both employees and external contractors. Whether you consider self-taught individuals or certified professionals, there are no guarantees that you can find a technically competent and honest person to perform your IT work. Wouldn't it be nice if the certifications had a way to measure the integrity of an individual or company?

Discussion Questions

1. Using a source such as *U.S. News and World Reports*, the AITP, or another reputable source, which colleges or universities would you look for prospective employees from? Why do these sources stand out from those from which you would not accept candidates?

2. Research the actual cost of the different certifications listed in the text and what exams have to be passed. Then compare these facts with the salaries offered on popular employment Web sites such as www.monster.com, www.dice.com, and www.salary.com. Which certifications have the greatest return on investment (ROI)? One way to calculate this is by using the following formula: ROI = First year salary/Cost of investment.

3. Contact one service provider, interviewing them on how they set themselves apart from others in the same area. What do they specialize in? What certifications, education, and experience do their employees have? What do they look for in a prospective employee?

Networking Technician Needs

A

Typical Component	Prices
RJ-45 crimpers	$30.00
Cat5 cable stripper	$10.00
Cabling tester	$150.00
Ethernet loopback tester	$10.00
Diagonal cutters	$15.00
Drywall hammer cutter	$23.00
Ultimate Tech toolbox	$40.00
Total cost	**$278.00**

Miscellaneous Components	
RJ-45 terminators (50 pack)	$30.00
RJ-45 strain relief (50 pack)	$9.00
RJ-45 dust covers	$0.49
RJ-45 protectors	$0.49
RJ-45 jacks (1 pack)	$4.00
Face plates (1 pack)	$2.50
In-wall cable boxes (10 pack)	$5.00
Zip tie assortment	$10.00
Total cost	**$61.48**

B

Visio Technical Drawing of the LAN Lab

Purpose

You will continue to develop skills documenting, researching, and diagramming a network using the Internet as a data source and the Visio drawing application.

Introduction

Documenting a network is a crucial task for any network designer or manager. Before beginning any major network design task, you should verify any existing drawings and documentation files.

This lab will strengthen your skills in quickly locating product information on network devices. You will also gain practice using the Visio drawing application to diagram and document the network in the lab.

Lab Activities

Part I: Orientation

1. Your instructor will give you a tour and orientation of the lab facilities. Take notes on paper during this process. Note the manufacturer and model number of all major pieces of networking equipment. Obtain the processor type and speed and basic installed hardware for each server and workstation in the lab.

2. Use the Internet to gather information about what each device is, its functionality, and so on.

Part II: Documentation

1. Using Visio or an equivalent drawing program, draw a physical representation of the LAN lab.

2. Clearly label and document appropriate lab equipment, its configuration, its cabling, and so on.

Deliverable

Print your file and save it for the final report for this laboratory. Make sure that your name or group members' names, course, and section information are shown on each page of all documents. You will need to be detailed when producing this document because you may will be needing it again in the future.

C

Cable
Manufacture
and Testing

Purpose

You will become familiar with the anatomy and installation of Category 5 or higher cable. This will include the manufacture of cross-connect and cross-over cables. We will be also be testing the efficiency of our manufacture. Another lesson learned is that it's much more cost-effective to purchase your cables than to manufacture your own.

Introduction

Networks are composed of computers, applications, CD-ROMs, Internet access, and transmission media. Several different types of cabling are in use today. These include copper cabling, fiber optic, and wireless media. Within each of these major categories, there are several subclasses. This laboratory deals with copper cabling, specifically Category 5 unshielded twisted pair (Cat5 UTP).

Currently Cat5 or Cat5e UTP is the cabling medium of choice in today's networking environment. (Cat6 is just not being installed in small to medium-sized companies at this time.) Fiber optic cable, composed of glass or plastic, has a much higher bandwidth capacity; but its installation costs and difficulty prohibit many organizations from implementing fiber optic. Cat5 cabling is composed of eight strands or four pairs of copper cabling that are twisted as pairs to keep the amount of interference down between pairs.

In this laboratory you will be performing several tasks that are common for WAN/LAN personnel. First you will be instructed on making up cross-connect or patch cables for connecting devices together or plugging into wall sockets. Next you will make cross-over cables. These are used to directly connect two PCs without having a signaling device such as a hub, similar to a null modem cable. After manufacturing the cables, we will be exploring the functionalities of an industry-standard network diagnostic and analytical tool.

Materials Needed

Two lengths of Category 5 cabling.

Four RJ-45 terminating ends.

One cable tester (either a continuity tester or a Fluke network analyzer).

One RJ-11 and RJ-45 crimp tool.

Lab Activities

Part I: Cross-Connect or Standard Patch Cable Manufacture

1. Obtain one length of Cat5 cable.
2. Make sure to cut off any existing terminator so that the cable ends are bare.

3. You will need to peel back about one inch of insulation, exposing the twisted pairs.

4. The colors of the four pairs are as follows:

   a. Blue (B) and white–blue (WB).

   b. Orange (O) and white–orange (WO).

   c. Green (G) and white–green (WG).

   d. Brown (Br) and white–brown (WBr).

5. After identifying the four different pairs of wires, spread the pairs out like a flower, with the pairs at the corners of an imaginary square encompassing the cable.

6. You will need to unwind the pairs while still keeping the pairs together during the rest of the manufacture.

7. Once you have separated the individual wires, you will need to straighten the wires so that they will fit properly into the guides in the terminators.

8. After the wires have been straightened, grab the ends of the cables between the thumb and forefinger of one hand and then move them around in a circular motion. This will straighten the wires and prepare them to slide into the terminator.

9. All of the wiring specifications will be given as though you are looking at the underside (or the side without the securing clip) of the RJ-45 terminator.

10. You will need to arrange the wires in the following order from left to right as you look at the bottom of the RJ-45 terminator:

Cross-Connect/Standard Patch	
End 1	**End 2**
White–orange	White–orange
Orange	Orange
White–green	White–green
Blue	Blue
White–blue	White–blue
Green	Green
White–brown	White–brown
Brown	Brown

11. Once the wires are arranged in the proper orientation, cut off the eight wires exactly square.

12. Insert the wires into the terminator so that the copper wires are visible through the end of the terminator.

13. Insert the terminator into a telco crimper and squeeze the handles together to insert the contacts into the wires, making the connection.

14. Now crimp the other end to complete the cable.

Part II: Cross-Over Cable Manufacture

1. The manufacture of cross-over cables is essentially the same as the manufacture of cross-connect cables, with the exception of the individual wire placement.

2. Follow Steps 1-8 in Part 1.

3. The placement of the eight wires differs from the cross-connect cables as shown here:

Cross-Connect		Cross-Over	
End 1	End 2	End 1	End 2
White–orange	White–orange	White–orange	*White–green*
Orange	Orange	Orange	*Green*
White–green	White–green	White–green	*White–orange*
Blue	Blue	Blue	Blue
White–blue	White–blue	White–blue	White–blue
Green	Green	Green	*Orange*
White–brown	White–brown	White–brown	White-brown
Brown	Brown	Brown	Brown

Note: These wires are as seen from underneath the RG-45 terminator! It does make a difference!

Part III: Punch-Down/Wall Socket Installation

1. The installation of any wire, especially Cat5 cabling, is one of the most common tasks performed by a telecommunications professional.

2. The first step is to strip off the outer jacket as before and separate the pairs of wires.

3. Next straighten the individual wires and place them into the wall socket in the correct order (the "B" standard).

4. These will be pushed into the channels and then punched down with a screwdriver. The traditional punch-down tool is too thick to use in this installation.

5. After punching down the wires, connect the known and good cross-connect cables to the Fluke OneTouch. The free ends will be plugged into the sockets you have just punched down.

6. When the Auto Test has been performed, the screen should confirm that you have created a "straight cable."

Cable Testing

1. Go to the instructor and check out a Fluke OneTouch Series II Network Assistant (or equivalent).

2. When handling the Fluke meter, be extremely careful! This particular piece of equipment costs about $5,000.

3. The Fluke meter consists of a gray handheld box with a yellow protective holder. You will be able to input with a touch screen.

4. Turn on the Fluke meter by pressing the green button located in the lower right corner of the meter. As the meter comes on, you will notice four orange lights that flash and a series of clicks and beeps.

5. The Fluke OneTouch series has such a wide range of functionality that there is actually a certification available from Fluke for the use of this product.

6. We are going to use only a small fraction of its capabilities.

7. You will notice several "file folder" icons such as Auto Test, Network Health, Cable Tests, and so on.

8. Plug both ends of your cross-connect cable into the two sockets on the Fluke.

9. Once the ends are connected, press the Auto Test icon. If your manufacture was successful, you will see the length of your cable and whether it is a straight cable or cross-over cable.

10. After you have a successful result, test your cross-over cable as well.

11. After you have finished with the Fluke, make sure to unplug all of the cabling, turn off the meter by pressing the green power button, and turn the meter back over to the instructor.

Deliverable

Before leaving the laboratory, be sure to have your instructor verify that the cross-connect/patch, cross-over, and punch-down tested successfully.

_____/_____

Cross-connect/patch   **Instructor signature   Date**

_____/_____

Cross-over cable   **Instructor signature   Date**

D

Introduction to the Fluke OneTouch Series II Network Assistant

Purpose

The purpose of this laboratory is to introduce you to network and physical layer analysis. Once the wiring has been installed into a facility, it becomes difficult to determine where, when, or even if there is an issue of network health or cabling. Many software publishers purport to have solutions to help determine and manage your network infrastructure. These solutions are certainly easy to introduce and implement, but without a well-established and stable physical layer, you cannot gather information if a cable fault is present. In short, a Layer 1 diagnostic tool is essential for network health and growth.

With the ability to easily and definitively obtain information about the network architecture, the network administrator or manager has more data with which to maintain the existing network. These data also allow more effective asset management of existing inventories and more effectively planning and budgeting for the foreseeable future.

Introduction

The Fluke OneTouch Series II Network Analyst is a sophisticated piece of diagnostic hardware able to determine faults in Layers 1 through 3. The Layers 1 and 2 capabilities consist of physical circuitry, electronic continuity, and physical or MAC addressing. Layer 3 begins the foray into logical addressing, network routing, and the protocol components of the OSI. A simple Layer 1 meter or pulse cable tester typically costs from $50 to $100 as opposed to several thousand dollars for a Layer 3 meter such as the OneTouch Analyst. How can the cost of such a tool be justified?

Lab Activities

Part I: Orientation

1. Familiarize yourself with the basic capabilities of the Fluke OneTouch Series II Network Assistant.

2. Access the Fluke Networks Web site at the following URL: http://www. flukenetworks.com.

3. Once there, you will need to find the page that compares and contrasts the different networking analysis tools that Fluke currently produces.

4. Find the information about the capabilities of the OneTouch. List the capabilities here. Later you will need this list to describe why each of its capabilities would be beneficial to a network administrator or manager.

Capabilities: _____

_____

_____

_____

_____

_____

5. Click on the link to the OneTouch Series II or go to the following URL. This page delineates the marketing data provided by the manufacturer about its product: http://www.flukenetworks.com/us/LAN/Handheld+Testers/ OneTouch+Series+II/Overview.htm.

6. Once you are familiar with this page, click on the following URL to become part of a live interactive demo. This page is almost like an interactive tutorial of how the product operates and the navigation through the screens and features. You will also notice explanations for most of the measurements that can be gathered with this particular analyst: http://www.flukenetworks. com/us/LAN/Handheld+Testers/OneTouch+Series+II/_see+it+live.htm.

Part II: Working with the OneTouch

1. Your lab group will need to check out a Fluke OneTouch Series II Network Assistant and a cross-connect/patch cable from the instructor. Be sure to get a cable that's long enough so you can be a comfortable distance from the hub while working.

2. Plug one end of the cross-connect cable into the leftmost port (when looking at the front of the meter) and the other end into an empty port on a hub.

3. At any time during this laboratory, you can go back to the online demo or the help menu to receive assistance.

4. Press the green button on the lower right of the screen to turn the unit on.

5. Once the unit is powered on, you will come to the main menu with the following main options:

   a. *Auto Test.*

   b. *Network Health.*

   c. *Cable Tests.*

   d. *NIC/Hub Tests.*

   e. *Connectivity Tests.*

   f. *Setup.*

6. We will walk through each of these menus in order. At any time you can use the back arrow to go up a level and readjust your plan of attack.

7. When *Auto Test* is pressed, a link pulse will be sent out to the network. You will begin to see how many NetWare servers, NetBIOS servers, subnets, workstations, printers, and the like there are on the network. After allowing this information to accumulate for a brief period, press the back button and return to the main menu.

8. Select the *Network Health* option. You will see a set of six gauges that measure percentage of network utilization (*% Util*), percentage of error (*% Error*), percentage of collision (*% Colsn*), percentage of broadcast (*% Bcast*), percentage of TCP/IP traffic (*% IPX*), and number of workstations (*Stns*).

9. Allow the analyst to collect data for approximately five minutes.

   What is the percentage of network utilization?   _____

   What is the percentage of error?   _____

   What is the percentage of collision?   _____

   What is the percentage of broadcast?   _____

   What is the percentage of TCP/IP?   _____

   What is the number of workstations?   _____

   Do these numbers change? If so, do they change frequently? Why or why not?

   _____

   _____

   _____

10. Other options from this screen are as follows:
    a. By selecting the *fps* option you will be able to determine the number of frames sent per second.
    b. The *Tab* shows a statistical analysis of the information gathered in "gauge view" in chart form.
    c. The *Map* selection brings us back to the same screen as seen in Step 8.

11. The *Cable Test* brings up the following submenus:
    a. *Cable Autotest.*
    b. *Wiremap Cable.*
    c. *Toner.*
    d. *Fiber.*
    e. *Define Cable CAT 5/5e.*

12. The *Cable Autotest* will not be available while one end of the cable is connected to something other than the second port of the OneTouch.

13. The *Wiremap Cable* also does not function correctly without a toner on the other end of the network.

14. The *Toner* configures for the high or low warbles for the toner frequency.

15. Because we don't have fiber cabling, the *Fiber* submenu will be unavailable.

16. You can configure the type of wire to be tested under the *Define Cable CAT 5/5e.*

17. The *NIC/Hub Tests:*
    a. *NIC Autotest.*
    b. *Hub Autotest.*
    c. *NIC Detector.*
    d. *Flash Hub Port.*

18. The *NIC Autotest* and *NIC Detector* analyses perform tests for the presence of and the connectivity of the NIC as opposed to just using the operating system (OS) utilities.

19. The *Hub Autotest* measures the network capabilities of the hub/switch you are attached to.

20. By using the *Flash Hub Port,* you can find in which port the cable you are connected into is actually located on the hub.

21. The next option on the main menu is *Connectivity Tests.* These are some of the most sophisticated analyses available on this analyst. These analyses are performed primarily in Layer 3 of the OSI. When you select *Connectivity Tests* the following submenu appears:
    a. *IP and SNMP Config.*
    b. *IP & NetWare Ping.*
    c. *Key Device Ping.*
    d. *Config Master.*
    e. *Station Locator.*
    f. *Internetwork.*

22. The *IP and SNMP Config* allows you to configure how the OneTouch is able to obtain an IP address—whether it's statically assigned or dynamically assigned. Also, the ability to configure the SNMP component of the network is invaluable when querying networking devices that are remote to the OneTouch.

23. The only true test of connectivity through TCP/IP or IPX/SPX is to send out an ICMP packet through the *IP & NetWare Ping.* The ping utility sends out an ICMP packet that is echoed from the IP address back to the originating device. A response usually contains an acknowledgment of a physical connection, the speed of the connection, and the logical address of the device.

24. You also have the ability to do a **Key Device Ping.** This lets you test for specific devices based not on their logical or network addresses but on their specific functions such as domain servers, Web servers, test servers, switches, and routers.

25. The **Station Locator (with IP)** helps to correspond the logical diagram and the physical diagram. This is especially useful in conjunction with Fluke's Visio-integrated network mapping software.

26. The **Internetwork Throughput Option** measures much of the same functions as the **Network Health** function.

27. The **Traffic Generator** puts out predetermined network traffic to show how the network responds to an increased load, thereby simulating adding more users or systems to the network. This can be helpful when comparing a baseline to a proposed corporate expansion, which allows for a proactive response before a failure.

Deliverable

1. What three network analyses would be most useful for you as a network administrator or manager? Defend your answers. Each of your answers should be at least a paragraph in length.

2. What network analysis tools not found in the OneTouch would you want in your network tool kit?

3. Using the materials and skills learned in the previous lab(s), what specific tools, skills, and analyses would you use to quickly and effectively troubleshoot your network?

4. Which measures would be useful for obtaining a baseline of network health? Provide at least three measures that should be used and explain why these measures would be included.

5. If you are currently working in a network environment without established documentation or a troubleshooting regimen, how would you write the regimen for documentation and troubleshooting of the Layer 1 through Layer 3 components and capabilities? What specific pieces of data would you collect for your environment? How often would these be reviewed and updated? What analyses would you use when to determine when, where, and how a problem occurred? How would these prove useful?

Network Cable
Verification
Form

Project name: _____

Client name: _____

Location: _____

Original installer: _____

Terminator 1:   _____

Terminator 2:   _____

Cable run: _____

Method used: _____

_____

_____

Cable certified: Yes   No

Cable tester used: _____

Certification criteria: _____

Additional documentation: _____

Cable tester: _____   **Date:** _____

Suggested Readings

As an IT professional, you will need an ever-expanding library of reference materials. Besides the initial cost of stocking this technical library, your library will need continual updating. Unfortunately, because of the changing nature of our industry, we have to purchase our materials when they cost the most, keep them while they depreciate fastest, and then try to sell them for a mere fraction of what we paid for them.

Here I have listed the references on my own shelf that I go to whenever I need to look something up or get some clarification. Some of these are a little old, but they still do a good job.

Dean, Tamara. *Network+ Guide to Networks* (4th ed.). Course Technology, 2006, ISBN 0-619-21743-X.

Dunsmore, Bradley, and Toby Skandier. *Telecommunications Technologies Reference*. Cisco Press, 2003, ISBN 1-58705-036-6.

Freeland, Curt, and Dwight McKay. *The Complete Systems Administrator*. OnWord Press, 2003, ISBN 0-7668-3519-7.

Goldman, James E., and Phillip T. Rawlings. *Local Area Networks: A Business-Oriented Approach* (2nd ed.). Wiley, 2000, ISBN 0471330477.

Green, James Harry. *The Irwin Handbook of Telecommunications* (4th ed.). McGraw-Hill, 2000, ISBN 0-07-135554-5.

Newton, Harry. *Newton's Telecom Dictionary* (16th ed.). CMP Books, 2000, ISBN 1-57820-053-9.

Wooten, Bob. *Building and Managing a World Class IT Help Desk*. Osborne/McGraw-Hill, 2001, ISBN 0-07-213237-X.

Glossary

A

access point Typically refers to a wireless access point or device that allows wireless users either public (uncontrolled access available to everyone regardless of security clearance) or private (controlled by security or organizational affiliation) access to a network.

analog signal A waveform consisting of audible sounds of a natural or non–computer-generated audio sound. When viewed on an oscilloscope, the waveform appears rounded as opposed to the more square waveform of digital or computer-generated waves.

application Typically refers to a software program such as an Internet browser, spreadsheet, word processor, or the like.

application layer Layer 7 of the OSI model. The application layer defines the user interface to the underlying network. For our purposes, any user interaction that allows typing and/or mouse-clicking would be considered an application layer function.

applications—needed and/or existing The second analysis to be performed in a business and technology analysis (BTA). The applications either are currently installed and considered "legacy" software that must be maintained or are new software that will be needed to help the organization function at a higher level. When the actual BTA is compiled and reported, applications are usually listed in broad generic terms such as *office productivity software* instead of specifically naming a particular product such as *Microsoft Office XP.*

B

bandwidth (1) Technically, all the frequencies for a communications transmission that are available for a particular network medium or service at a specific moment. (2) Generally, the amount of network traffic that can be transmitted through a given network at a given time.

baseband Transmissions that utilize the full amount of bandwidth for a single type of communications. Examples would be analog telephone service or dial-up networking.

broadband Transmissions that utilize only part of the overall bandwidth for individual communications. Examples include DSL, analog and digital cable, and so on.

business and technology analysis or BTA Defined and published by James E. Goldman and Phillip T. Rawlings in *Local Area Networks: A Business-Oriented Approach*

(ISBN 0471330477), a BTA is a process by which companies (and IT professionals) can begin with the goals of the organization and work toward the means by which the IT staff would be able to fulfill those goals.

business needs and budget   The first analysis performed in a BTA report. The overall business goals of the organization should be the primary determinant guiding the BTA process. While some companies have a one-year, three-year, or even five-year business plan, others do not. The more forward-looking the business, the more likely the IT staff can fulfill their duties. Additionally, the available budget should be determined for more accurate forecasting.

C

cable   Although *cable* can be generically used to describe any network medium, the term typically refers to either coaxial cable (such as for A/V transmissions) or twisted pair cabling (for standard network transmissions).

circuit   A circuit, in its simplest form, is a metal wire (usually copper) that is connected to both the "+" or positive side of a power source and the "−" or negative side of the same power source. This allows the energy to flow from the positive end of the power source into its negative end. If there is a break in the circuit, the circuit has a "short." This is important to networking because if a resource has no connection to the network, no communications will be sent. All network traffic is sent through electrical pulses (through copper), light waves or pulses (through fiber optic), or wireless transmission (through the air).

coaxial cable   Traditional A/V cabling used in home wiring for televisions, cable subscriptions, and satellite receivers. Although coaxial cable (coax) is known for its weather resistance, ease of termination, high degree of electrical shielding, and overall physical strength, its use has dwindled in favor of higher-bandwidth twisted pair and fiber optic cabling.

computer   A digital appliance with a CPU, local disk storage, and inputs and outputs.

CPE or customer premises equipment   CPE is equipment that belongs to the customer, not to the service provider.

cross talk   Cross talk is the phenomenon experienced when data cables are installed near other cables transmitting electricity. This can have a very detrimental effect on network throughput. It's not uncommon to experience intermittent but persistent communication errors when a data cable has been installed too close to an electrical wire or fixture, such as a fluorescent light fixture.

D

data format/traffic characteristics   The third analysis performed as a part of a BTA report. The amount of data that a company, or network segment, sends; the times, types, and quantities are the information needed to perform a proper traffic analysis.

digital signal A waveform consisting of electronically generated or synthetic sound. When viewed on an oscilloscope, the waveform appears square with distinct boundaries defining the signal, as opposed to the rounded waveform seen with analog or natural waves.

DSL Acronym for digital subscriber line. DSL is a misnomer because the service is actually an analog signal of a higher frequency than those used by voice communications.

E

Ethernet A PC-based LAN contention-based networking standard originally conceived by Robert Metcalf further developed by Digital, Intel, and Xerox. It became known as the DIX standard but is now officially designated as IEEE 802.3. There are many variants on the common Ethernet theme, each labeled as IEEE 802.3x.

F

fiber optic Cable medium made of ultrapure glass or plastic fibers. Used in high-speed network communications or where excess electrical interference or noise would make traditional copper cabling less desirable.

firewall A software application or hardware device (or combination of the two) that can allow network communications selective entry to and exit from the network.

H

hub A physical layer (OSI Layer 1) device used to connect multiple workstations, printers, servers, and the like together. Hubs can be thought of as networking "power strips" that broadcast all network traffic to all connected devices regardless of the data's intended recipient.

I

IEEE The Institute of Electrical and Electronics Engineers.

IEEE Project 802 The project that was started in February 1980 by the IEEE to establish networking standards. All standards that have been proposed, drafted, and released have the prefix *IEEE 802.x*.

Internet A collection of separate and distinct networks connected together with routers and using network layer (Layer 3 or logical) addresses. With an uppercase "I" the term is used for the World Wide Web or international Internet.

internet A collection of separate and distinct networks connected together with routers and using network layer (Layer 3 or logical) addresses. With a lower case "i" the term is used to define any internetwork other than the public Internet.

intranet   A private network wherein users can have Internet-like access to resources through a standard Web browser. Companies often use an intranet to post information that is to be kept within the organization, is housed on internal Web servers, but can be accessed through a standard Web browser.

L

LAN   An acronym for local area network. A LAN is a group of interconnected computing devices within a small geographic region such as an office, a building, or even a campus. The LAN is traditionally wholly owned by the organization that's using it.

logical address   An address that is not assigned based on a fixed or rigid physical location. Logical addresses are network (Layer 3) or protocol addresses such as TCP/IP addresses.

M

MAC address   Media access control address. Defined as a hardware, or firmware, level address assigned by the manufacturer, the MAC address is used by Layer 2 switches and bridges to identify both the sender and receiver systems.

N

network   Typically a collection of computers, printers, servers, and the like that are connected together to facilitate the sharing of files, printers, Internet access, and other resources that are not available on individual systems.

network topology   The overall design of the network architecture. There are two main types of topologies: physical and logical. Physical topology can be thought of as an actual depiction of how the network either will be installed or is currently installed. Logical topology is more of an engineer's conceptual view of how the network traffic will be sent from one point to another, without the clutter of putting all network devices and infrastructure in the diagram.

NIC or network interface card   The device that allows a computer system to communicate with the network cabling and available bandwidth.

O

OSI model   An industry-standard abstract concept or seven-layer model used in the development of new standards, the interaction of existing standards, and the support of legacy devices. The OSI model provides a logical framework or language that is used to describe the communication between two systems regardless of the hardware, software, operating system, communications protocol, or type of network connection.

P

packet   Data that have been broken into smaller pieces and packaged for network transmission by the transport layer. Technically a packet exists only in the transport and network layers before being converted to a frame in the data link layer.

physical address   MAC address.

protocol   Software, and occasionally hardware, that exist as a liaison between the network devices and the system are called protocols. Another way of looking at protocols is that they are the language for communicating across a network between different devices.

R

RJ-45   Registered Jack–45; used for terminating Categories 5, 5e, 6, 7, and so on twisted pair cabling for network communication. Many people think that RJ-45s look like very wide phone connectors.

router   An internetworking device possessing two or more separate network interfaces used to interconnect different network segments based on their Layer 3 (logical or protocol) addresses.

S

segmentation   The logical separation (using Layer 2 or above devices) of different network parts so that data communications are localized and overall traffic flows are broken up. Segmentation provides the means by which individual departments can be their own private networks in case of a network outage.

server   A centralized system with resources that can be shared or "served" to the individual workstations.

shielded twisted pair   A variant of twisted pair cabling with an aluminum shield wrapped around the copper wires to minimize electrical interference, cross talk, or electronic eavesdropping.

switch   Networking device, similar to a hub, used to connect systems together using either data link layer (physical) or network layer (logical) addresses. Because switches do not share bandwidth like Layer 1 devices, they are considerably more desirable than hubs at a comparable price.

T

technology—available   The final analysis to be performed in a BTA report. After exhaustive examination of the possible factors that will influence the technology selection, there should be a limited number of products, either hardware or software, available for use that suit the needs of the organization. Said another way, "At the end of the BTA, we should be talking apples and apples."

TCP/IP   A complete suite or set of protocols that evolved as a result of the development work by DARPA. TCP/IP is the default standard for modern networks and the Internet. Each of the protocols within TCP/IP performs functions, but the specifics are beyond the scope of this text.

twisted pair   Copper cabling that consists of pairs of individually insulated wires that have been twisted together to help minimize cross talk.

W

WAN   An acronym for wide area network. WANs were historically built and maintained by telephone providers and typically span large geographic areas. Network access to a WAN is usually on a subscription basis.

workstation   Generic term for an end user's computer system.

Index

A

A+ Certified Service
Technician, 175–176
Access method architecture,
55
Access point, defined, 199
Accountability, and customer
focus, with nonprofit, 95
Accounting documents,
42–43
Active Directory Services
(Microsoft), and
security, 97
Adversarial upgrades, 165
Advisor software (Belarc), 45,
158–160
Amplifiers, 16, 28–30
Analog signals
and amplifiers, 16
defined, 199
Application(s)
defined, 199
recommending specific, 56
Application layer
defined, 199
and e-mail, 11–12
Applications, needed or existing,
54–55, 57, 82, 85, 107,
110, 117
defined, 199
pivotal nature of, 77
Architecture, 36–38
and BTA, 55–58, 83,
108, 111

experimental network, 118
office network, 118
Asset management (AM), 42, 50
and upgrades, 165–166
Attack, detecting, in sniffer,
149–150
Audience. *See* Customer
Audio signals, and amplifiers, 16
Automatic tools, 44–45
Auto Test, and Fluke OneTouch
Series II Network, 191–192

B

Backbone medium
Cat5e UTP cabling, 112
fiber optic, 99
Backup, configuring and testing,
104–105
Bandwidth (BW)
defined, 22–23, 199
and Fast Ethernet, 75
and hubs and switches, 96
latency in, 32
and media cost, 28
Baseband, defined, 199
Baseline analysis, 148–150
Belarc Advisor, 45, 158–160
Bid
lowest, pitfalls of, 66
official process, 67
sample, 88–89
waiting to submit, 56
Blueprints

hand-drawn, 94
and installation, 79
land plot, 75
office plan, 115
Bridges, 17, 31
Broadband, defined, 199
Brownfield network, 5
Budget
and BTA, 54, 57
defined, 200
Business conditions
basic, 114–116
considerations, 73–74,
94–95
Business needs
addressed in BTA, 54, 57, 82,
85, 107, 110, 117
defined, 200
Business and technology
analysis (BTA)
defined, 199
and design phase, 65–66
detailed discussion, 96–98
detailed recommendations,
74–77
internal use, 60
introduction, 52–54
process, 53–57
submitting two versions, 72,
107–112
Business and technology analysis (BTA), examples, 57–59,
117–119
final drafts, 85–87, 107–112